Between Two Worlds

Between Two Worlds

Autobiography of a
Child Survivor
of the Holocaust

R. Gabriele S. Silten

FITHIAN PRESS, SANTA BARBARA • 1995

Published by Fithian Press
A Division of Daniel and Daniel, Publishers, Inc.
Post Office Box 1525
Santa Barbara, CA 93102

LIBRARY OF CONGRESS CATALOGING-IN-PUBLICATION DATA
  Silten, R. Gabriele S.
    Between two worlds : autobiography of a child survivor of the holocaust /
  R. Gabriele S. Silten.
      p.   cm.
    Includes bibliographical references.
    ISBN 1-56474-126-5
    1. Silten, R. Gabriele S.—Childhood and youth. 2. Holocaust, Jewish (1939–
  1945)—Personal narratives. 3. Terezín (Czech Republic : Concentration camp).
  I. Title
  D804.3.S5848   1995
  940.53'18'092—dc20
    [B]   94-40458
                                                            CIP

*For Hans, specifically,
and for the other one and one-half million
children who were not as lucky as I;
they were murdered, but I lived.*

Acknowledgements

A very big thank you is due to a number of people who have been of enormous help in this undertaking: to Maryon Leonard, who edited, proofread, and gave suggestions and lots of encouragement; to Dr. Sarah Moskovitz, who helped me tap into my child voice, and without whom this book would never have been written; to Harriett Covey and Zee Arnold, who also read this work and gave suggestions; to my cousins Werner and John Hasenberg, who took a number of photos for me of Theresienstadt as it is today; and to Mariana Cheng, talented artist, who made the cover drawing for me. To all of you, my family and friends, go my warmest thanks and hugs.

Contents

Foreword 13
Prologue 17

Berlin, 1933-1938
    The Beginning 23

Amsterdam, 1938-1943
    Departure 29
    The Boarding House 31
    Our Apartment 33
    Routines, Outings, and Games 35
    Omi Comes 38
    School 42
    Tensions in the House 46
    Invasion 47
    My Friend Max 49
    My Eighth Birthday 51
    New Rules 54
    The Yellow Star 59
    Unusual Lessons 62
    The Sandals and Other Worries 65
    Black-Outs and Window Tapes 67
    The *Knijpkat* 70
    Pick-Ups 71
    Deportation 76

Westerbork, June 20, 1943-January 18, 1944
    Arrival in the Camp and the Barracks 81
    Westerbork: Location and Description 86
    Work and Food 92
    Games 94
    Tensions and Lessons 96
    Illness and Death 98
    A Walk and a Drawing 101
    Showers and Noise 103
    We Leave Westerbork 105

Theresienstadt, January 20, 1944–June 1945

Theresienstadt: History and Description 109
Transport and Arrival 113
Hans and I 118
Food 122
Other Games 124
My Four Companions 126
Daily Activities 129
My Eleventh Birthday 135
Two Jobs 138
I Am Ill Again 142
My Nightgown and Other Clothes 146
I Learn to Read German 151
Mami Is in the Hospital 153
The Beautification 156
The Film 159
The Making of the Film 161
After the Film 164
Tommy 168
Winter 1944 170
The Russians Are There 173
My Twelfth Birthday 176
Return to Holland 179
Eindhoven 182
Return to Amsterdam 184
After the War 187
Epilogue 190

What Happened to Whom? 195
Glossary 199
Notes 203

ERNST SILTEN
B. Apr. 22, 1866
D. Mar 5, 1943

MARTA SILTEN
(NÉE FRIEDBERG)
B. Oct. 12, 1877
D. July 7, 1943

RICHARD TEPPICH
B. Jun. 27, 1869
D. July 18, 1931

GERTRUD TEPPICH
(NÉE HERZ)
B. Feb. 12, 1880
D. Nov. 18, 1942

Married May 15, 1900   *Married Oct. 14, 1903*

HEINZ SILTEN
B. June 11, 1901
D. Mar. 13, 1953

FRITZ SILTEN
B. Feb. 16, 1904
D. Nov. 5, 1980

ILSE SILTEN
(NÉE TEPPICH)
B. Feb. 23, 1909
D. Feb. 23, 1977

URSULA (ULLE)
TEPPICH
B. Dec. 6, 1914
D. May 5, 1990

Married August 6, 1931

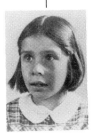

RUTH GABRIELE
SARAH SILTEN
B. May 30, 1933

Foreword

My childhood and early teen years were spent in a sort of twilight zone. This book is a going back in time and space to recapture what happened to me and thereby make my story public in an effort to do my small part to try to ensure that this type of genocide will never happen again.

I have relied principally on my own memory of events, a memory which, for better or worse, is very good. For some few dates and some special details I have drawn on a small number of books, a list of which can be found at the end of this autobiography. The copies of documents contained herein were made from those which my father was able to keep and which are now in my possession. Photographs of Westerbork and copies of some documents are courtesy of the Bureau for War Documentation in Amsterdam, Holland. For the sake of clarity, I have translated, as best I could, all measurements which were in meters into yards and feet.

All of this happened a long time ago, of course, but it is as clear as though it happened yesterday. As the child I was then, I saw things in a different way than the adults saw them, and I have tried to bring that out through passages from a child's point of view written in the present tense. I existed between adulthood and childhood, between the normal and the abnormal, between the real and the unreal, an existence between two worlds.

Between Two Worlds

Prologue

My family had lived in Germany for generations; our genealogical chart goes back to the 1600s. The first person of our family to settle in Berlin received permission to do so in the early 1800s, when the first Jews were allowed to live there. Both my maternal and paternal grandmothers were born in Berlin; my two grandfathers were born in Koenigsberg when that city was still in Prussia.

My maternal grandfather, Richard Teppich, did a variety of things to earn a living; among other businesses he founded at various times was a dry cleaning establishment. I never knew him; he died in 1931, the year my parents were married. In photographs he is almost always shown with a yachting cap on: he loved his boat and the idea of being on the water. His wife, Gertrud Teppich, née Herz, my Omi Trudl, was a homemaker, as was the custom then. They had three children, all girls, of whom the oldest, Anita, died very young at age eight. The other two were Ursula, called Ulle for short, who was born in 1914, and the eldest, Ilse, born in 1909, who was my mother. The family lived on Luisenstrasse in Berlin. An "assimilated" family, they kept no Jewish laws or holidays and did not go to synagogue. Both my grandfather and grandmother had several siblings: my grandfather had two sisters and several brothers, and Omi Trudl had two brothers, Max and Eugen.

On the other side of the family, my paternal grandfather, Dr. Ernst Silten, my Opa Ernst, had studied pharmacology and received his Ph.D. in 1895. He had worked as an apprentice pharmacist in many pharmacies in Germany, as was then the custom, and had finally settled in Berlin. He was one of five sons, and his four brothers also eventually settled in Berlin. My grandmother, Marta Silten, née Friedberg, was one of three sisters. She and my grandfather were married in 1900. Their eldest son, my Uncle Heinz (later Henry), was born in 1901, and their second son, Fritz, my father, was born in 1904. Like my mother's family, the Siltens were also assimilated Jews who kept no dietary laws, did not go to synagogue or observe Jewish holidays, and knew little if anything about Judaism.

My grandfather owned his pharmacy, the Kaiser Friedrich Apotheke, as well as a factory where he produced not only pharmaceuticals but also oxygen for use in hospitals. The pharmacy was on Karlstrasse, and my grandfather also owned the building in which it was housed. The pharmacy was on the ground floor, the factory on the second floor (or "first," as it is called in Europe), offices on the third floor, and the family lived on the fourth floor. My father followed in his father's footsteps, studying pharmacology and earning his Ph.D. in 1930. He worked in his father's pharmacy beginning in 1922, first as an apprentice, later as a partner.

I remember the apartments of both sets of grandparents as large and very comfortable. Both families were comfortably well off, my father's family more so than my mother's, and both could afford to hire domestic help. Omi Trudl employed a cook, who was actually a general factotum and who helped her enormously in a number of ways, especially after the laws against Jews went into effect. My father's parents employed a housekeeper who, after my grandmother had left for Holland, stayed with my grandfather and helped him all she could. In 1938 my grandfather was forced to sell his pharmacy— most if not all Jewish-owned businesses likewise underwent forced sale at that time—and he had to survive as best he could.

My father, my mother, and I fled Berlin in 1938 and went to Amsterdam, Holland, where my Omi Marta joined us in 1939. My

Uncle Heinz had gone to England in the early 30s, and my Aunt Ulle went to Switzerland in 1938. My parents' first cousins were able to flee to England, Denmark, and Argentina when that was still possible. None of my grandparents survived the Holocaust; the two who remained in Berlin committed suicide rather than be deported to Auschwitz; Omi Marta, who had joined us in Holland, committed suicide in the concentration camp Westerbork rather than be deported to Auschwitz. All of my great-aunts and great-uncles as well as most of their children were murdered by the Nazis. My parents and I, by great good luck, stayed together during the war and survived together. Uncle Henry died in 1953, my mother in 1977, my father in 1980, and Aunt Ulle in 1990.

LEFT: *My grandfather Richard Teppich with his bride, Gertrud, in 1903. Richard was thirty-four years old; Gertrud was 23.*

RIGHT: *My grandfather Ernst Silten with his bride, Marta, in 1899. Ernst was thirty-three years old; Marta was 22.*

Berlin

1933-1938

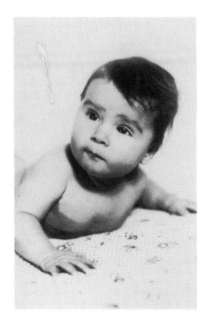

Gabriele at eleven months

The Beginning

A child's bedroom: in it a small crib with bars on one side, white or beige. A high table covered with a piece of white cloth. I lie on the table, on my stomach, nude. I'm being held by two hands—warm hands. My mother? I struggle, wriggle my arms, kick my legs and cry, mouth wide open. Another big person touches me with something cold. A doctor? He puts his instrument in my behind. It feels cold and I'm frightened, so I protest more and more loudly. It doesn't do any good, though. I'm helpless and unhappy. I am one year old.

Another bedroom, in my grandparents' house. I am in bed, snuggled under the blankets. A lady comes in and picks me up out of bed. She carries me out of the room into the hallway. There are others in the hall as well. I smell smoke and see the blackened ceiling of the hall. I am two years old.

A room in my other grandmother's house. There are a couch, a low table, and an easy chair covered with flowered plush, a velvety material. On the table is a large model of a ship made by my grandfather. I am allowed to play with it, though no one else is allowed to touch it. There are small stuffed dogs in the room as well—my mother's toys from when she was a little girl. I take them from the couch, put them on the ship, and they take a voyage. I am three years old.

•

My grandfather's pharmaceutical factory. I stand on a chair at a long counter next to my father and grandfather. I shake a small brown glass bottle with a cork in it from side to side. My father shakes a larger one and my grandfather an even larger one. We all make the same movement at the same time—three generations of pharmacists. My grandfather praises me for being so helpful. I am three years old.

A park with many trees and wide gravelled paths. My grandmother takes me for a walk. There are many people, so my grandmother holds me by the hand. I'm not allowed to walk on my own; I might get lost. Omi has a gray Bedlington terrier named Piet who is allowed to run loose in the park and explore all he wants. I watch him interestedly as he runs and plays. I am four years old.

Unconnected, vividly colored, kaleidoscopic images: my earliest memories.

•

I was born in Berlin, Germany, in 1933, the same year in which Hitler became chancellor. It was neither a very good birth present nor a very good omen, since I was born into a Jewish family whose members on both sides of the family had lived in Germany for generations. My memories of my first five years are disconnected: I remember a red carpet on the stairs of our apartment, a heavy buffet in our dining room, some easy chairs in our living room. I remember high ceilings in Opa Ernst's and Omi Marta's apartment, tall chairs in many colors (many years later I learned they were Gobelin chairs), a large kitchen in Omi Trudl's apartment where the cook always welcomed me with a treat. We went on a summer vacation somewhere in the country to a house named Klado, where friends came to visit us. I had a favorite doll, a teddy bear, and other toys. It was a comfortable life for a small child, with lots of family members

Omi Marta with Piet in the park.

to play with and spoil me—grandparents, cousins of my parents, my uncle, my aunt. I remember no tension, anxiety, or upheavals, though they must have existed for the adults.

After my fifth birthday the situation began to change. I turned five in May of 1938. It was the first birthday on which my father was absent. On June 15 of that year, in order to flee Nazism, my mother and I left Berlin to follow my father to Holland, where he had gone earlier in the year to find a place to work and prepare for our coming. In order to leave Germany for a safer place, my parents had to leave behind everybody and everything that was dear to them. They left their parents, they left other family as well as friends, they left their home and most of their possessions. They left their birthplace, their language, and their past, and they left behind their once-bright future.

ABOVE: *Gabriele at age three on vacation at the house "Klado."*
BELOW: *Gabriele at age four with mother (right) and Aunt Ulle.*

Amsterdam

1938-1943

Departure

I don't remember everything of that journey to Holland. Accompanied by my grandparents, a tall man with white hair and dark clothes, a stately lady dressed in black, and a slightly smaller lady with a large hat, we go to a train station where the train, a big black monster snorting smoke like a dragon, stands waiting. We stand on the platform, rather silent. I hold Mami's hand. Every once in a while one of my Omis or my Opa picks me up or hugs me without saying anything. Our suitcases are already on the train. The only one who isn't with us is Papi. He left a long time ago, and we haven't seen him or spoken to him since. Mami says that we'll see him soon.

Mami, Mami! Mami, why does it growl? Does it bite? Mami, why is there smoke? Mami, it's not going to leave without us, is it? It sounds impatient! It wants to go! Why don't we get in? Are you sure it's not leaving without us? Mami, I'm scared!

•

My mother and my grandparents paid no attention to me and my worries. What did my mother feel at that moment? Surely she was afraid also, going into the unknown with a small child, not guessing what awaited her, having a hard time saying goodbye to her mother, parents-in-law, and all she knew and loved.

The train did not leave without us, of course, but no one ever did reassure me that it wouldn't. I remember a ship as well. Where or when we embarked and where it went has escaped my memory. Eventually we reached Lugano, Switzerland, where we spent a month with my Aunt Ulle, my mother's sister, who had been sent there by her company to work and who was to spend the rest of her life there. After that month we somehow made our way to Amsterdam, arriving there on July 21, 1938. We did not yet speak Dutch, of course, nor did we have our own apartment or anybody with whom we might stay. So we found a room in a boarding house and lived there until November 17, 1938.

Map of the Netherlands as sent to me by the Netherlands Tourist Board.
I have added Concentration Camp Westerbork
and circled both it and Amsterdam.

The Boarding House

I only vaguely remember my father being there during our four months in the boarding house. During the day, naturally, he was gone to his office. My mother was often gone as well, to look for an apartment. I was left in the care of the landlady, who was also to feed me. I was bored and unhappy and afraid of being abandoned. There is one day I particularly remember:

•

I do not want my mother to leave, and I scream at the top of my lungs.

No, no, don't go away! I want to go with you! Don't leave me! Mami! Maaaaamiiii!

Big tears stream down my cheeks, I stamp my feet and swing my small fists, but it changes nothing at all: my mother leaves all the same, and I am inconsolable. When lunchtime comes the landlady tries to persuade me to eat. She speaks only Dutch and I speak only German, so our communication is not too effective. In any event, I refuse to eat my lunch, and nothing she does is of any use.

No, I don't want it, I don't like it. I want my Mami! I don't want you! I don't want to eat. I want my Mami! Mami, where are you?

I end up trying to eat only the pudding, which is meant for dessert. Since I stick my spinachy fork in it, which leaves traces, this is very obvious, and when my mother returns later on, I am scolded again for not wanting to eat, trying to eat my dessert only, and in general for having been a bad girl.

·

I was made to eat things I neither knew nor liked, I didn't understand the language, I was out of my familiar surroundings, and I was
being left with strangers. I felt abandoned, lost, and frightened because I could not understand what was happening and nobody even
tried to explain anything to me. For a five-year-old child it was a
terrible experience. I was very unhappy and I cried a lot.

Our Apartment

On November 17, 1938, we finally moved into our own apartment in an area called in Dutch "de Rivierenbuurt," the river neighborhood, because all the streets were named after rivers. Ours was a wide street named Noorder Amstellaan, North Amstel Lane. On our side of the street there was one long block of apartment houses which all looked alike, with stoops in front, more stairs to go up, and then a number of doors, each of which led to an apartment. Between the two sides of the street was a green belt, a sort of mini-park, with grass, bushes, and flowers. Along it ran the *"tramrails,"* rails for the streetcar, which at that time went in the opposite direction of other traffic.

It wasn't "our" apartment in the sense of ownership; it was rented, as were all the apartments on that street and in Holland generally. Families did not usually own their own home or apartment. We lived on the third floor—what is called the second floor in Europe. There were apartments below and above us, and one on the street level. It was a big apartment: living room, dining room, two bedrooms, kitchen, and bathroom. The living room was a comfortable room with deep easy chairs made of what looked like brown leather and perhaps was. There was a rectangular coffee table which had a map of the stars and planets on top under a glass plate with sharp corners. I have good reason to remember that: I hit my head on those corners many times when I was very small. The dining room was a difficult room for a small child: the table was very high, as were the chairs, and I had trouble climbing up on them. The larger bedroom was my parents'. It had greenish furniture: a big double bed, two wardrobes, and nightstands and a chair or two. My own room, *de kinderkamer*, the child's room, was also large, although not as large as my parents' room. It had a bed that folded up into a bedstead which was fastened to the wall. In Dutch it was called an *opklapbed*, literally a "flip-up bed." In order to "hide" the bed, the bedstead had curtains in front of it, light blue with tiny flowers, which were drawn during the day. I also had a little round cream-colored table with a matching chair, and under the window stood two bookcases for all my books. I was a bookworm even then! Against the other wall stood a couch, and the room had a built-in closet as well as a wash basin. The hanging lamp did not have a shade; instead it had a blue wooden ring around it, on which were sawn-out and painted figures from fairy tales. Snow White and the seven dwarfs were there, Little Red Ridinghood and the wolf, Hansel and Gretel and their gingerbread house, and others. At night, when I was in bed, I imagined that these figures might come alive and play in my room or even play with me. That was exciting.

Our apartment (marked with X) in Noorder Amstellaan.

Routines, Outings, and Games

Slowly but surely a routine is established. We make the acquaintance of the family who lives in the apartment above ours and who has two little girls. Willy, the elder one, is two or three years older than I; Carla, the younger one, is six months younger than I. The first meeting between Carla and me is not the gentlest, since neither can understand the other. Carla spits in my face in a fury that I do not speak as she does, and I retaliate by slapping her. Of course we both "know" that we are right. However, soon I am sent to the same Montessori kindergarten where Carla goes, and we become best friends very quickly. We do not learn any "academics" there—no ABCs, no reading, no numbers, or anything like that. We do learn to play together with a minimum of quarrels; we play in a sandbox outside, or we learn games inside. We learn songs. We learn to draw certain shapes, like circles or stars, and we learn to color them while staying within the lines. One day I cannot seem to manage to stay within the lines; my pencil seems to be alive and to go where it wants, outside the lines.

Oh, no, that doesn't look nice. Now what do I do? I know, I'll just go all around over the line, nice and even. That'll look just as good.

And, with my tongue between my lips, I do just that. When the teacher sees it, however, she does not approve at all, and I feel very frustrated because I have worked very hard to make it neat!

•

Not having a front or back yard, Carla and I also played in the street with the other children who lived on our block. We played the usual children's games: hopscotch, hide and seek, skipping rope, spinning top, marbles, and other games, all depending on the season. On the corner of Noorder Amstellaan and the next cross street, Maasstraat or Meuse Street, was a grocer's shop which sold coffee, tea, butter, sweets, and other such things. It was called Van Amerongen, and the manager was Mevrouw Gijtenbeek, Mrs. Gijtenbeek, a small blond woman who liked children and would give us sweets when we came in.

Carla and I also played in each other's apartments. One of our games was called *het apenspel,* the monkey game. It consisted of climbing on the bedstead or on top of the closet via the bedstead and then jumping from there down to the couch. This did not do the couch any good in the long run, of course, and my mother was anything but delighted by this particular game.

I also played at the house of my cousins Reni (Irene) and Werner, who lived two blocks away. Werner was five years older than I, and I don't really remember actually playing with him. He was far too grown up to be bothered with anyone as small as I. Reni was three years older than I, and we did play together. The two families took trips together as well, for example to Holland's highest "mountain," the Tafelberg, Table Mountain, which is all of 200 feet high. On summer Sundays, when the weather was warm enough, my parents often took me to Zandvoort, a small beach town with a lovely, wide, sandy beach. My father helped me build castles, my mother played ball with me, I searched for shells, made sand cakes, and found other children to play with. On other weekends we might take a walk through the (manmade) wood near Amsterdam, the Amsterdamse Bos, where my father convinced me to search for Hansel's and Gretel's house.

We went to the circus when it came to town. It used to perform in a building called Carré. I thought the name of the circus was very funny: it was called Circus Knie—*knie* being the Dutch word for knee. We also began to follow some of the Dutch holiday traditions, for example the celebration of Sinterklaas, Saint Nicholas, which takes place on the eve and day of the saint's birthday, December 6. Before his birthday the good saint travels from Spain, where he lives, to Holland, usually by boat. He brings his white horse, which is his transportation once he has arrived in Holland, and he brings his helper, a Moor named Zwarte Piet, Black Peter. With his helper and his horse he travels over the roofs and sends Black Peter down the chimneys to put presents in the shoes of the children, which they have put out in readiness, usually with a carrot and some water for the horse or maybe a cookie for Sinterklaas. If the children have not been good, they do not get presents. Instead they receive a switch made of twigs. If they've been very bad they get put into the sack in which Zwarte Piet and Sinterklaas normally carry presents. They are then taken to Spain for a year to be taught manners. Even though Sinterklaas' birthday is on December 6, the shoes are put out on the evening of the fifth, so that the children find their presents on the sixth. It is also on the fifth that families celebrate at home, with presents and short verses attached to the presents describing either the present or an attribute of the recipient. Often the recipient has to guess what's in the package. It's a typically Dutch holiday, and since we now lived in Holland we joined in this celebration.

Omi Comes

In September of 1939 there was another upheaval. My parents told me that my Omi Marta was coming to live with us in Amsterdam. I called both my grandmothers "Omi"; their first names were used to distinguish them. Omi Marta was my father's mother; Omi Trudl (short for Gertrud) was my mother's mother. I never knew my Opa Richard, my mother's father, who died shortly before my parents got married. But my Opa Ernst, my father's father, I knew well.

I was not told just why Omi Marta was coming. Many years later I learned that Opa Ernst had insisted that she leave Berlin, saying that he would follow her (which he was never able to do), and so she set out to come to Amsterdam to live with her son, daughter-in-law, and granddaughter. How did she feel having to leave behind everything she knew? How did she manage to make the trip to Holland? Had she come by train? Had she come by boat, as we had done? How long had it taken her? Had she brought her furniture with her, or had she been able to ship it? I don't know the answers to any of those questions; when she joined us in Amsterdam I was just six years old and certainly not able to ask. Later, after the war, when I was older, the whole subject of the war years was never discussed, and I did not ask any questions. The fact remains that she arrived about a year after we had come to Amsterdam, in September of 1939.

Our apartment now changes considerably as Omi Marta has to be accommodated. What had been the dining room now also becomes her bedroom. The clearest thing in my memory of that bed/dining room is the picture hanging above the buffet. It is a large black-and-white picture of Napoleon on a horse. I do not know who he was but have been told his name, and the picture impresses me greatly. I practice pronouncing his name—Napoleon Bonaparte—every time I come into Omi Marta's room.

With only one bathroom in the apartment, as is the custom, and three adults plus one child to share it, Omi makes her morning toilet at the wash basin in my room. I am fascinated by her use of cleansing lotion and decide that when I grow up I will also use "milk" on my face. I love to observe Omi while she does this or while she combs and puts up her beautiful white hair, as I love to observe the adults in my world in general. Omi is a very handsome and imposing woman who wears her clothes with simple elegance. She keeps herself very straight and always behaves "as a lady should."

It is Omi Marta who teaches me a number of things. It is she who teaches me to eat with adult-sized utensils; she who teaches me to braid my doll Erika's long hair; she who teaches me my multiplication tables by making me repeat them, seated in one of her big chairs with my legs sticking out straight in front of me, until I know them by heart and practically without thinking. She draws for me and makes doll clothes for my dolls. She sews a green outfit for my teddy bear. It has little red buttons, and the sleeves, collar, and pocket are outlined in red. On the pocket she embroiders my bear's name, Brunette. To all this I add a yellow ribbon around her left ear (her hair is not long enough to tie a bow in), and I think her beautiful. Omi knits me a blue dress with matching underpants, and she knits a green suit for my doll Peter. It has three pieces: a sweater, a pair of pants, and a beret. (Later those three pieces will become very important.) For one of the other dolls she makes a pair of pajamas out of pink flannel with a flower pattern. It so resembles my own pajamas that even I, who believe wholeheartedly in Sinterklaas, wonder just how the good saint was able to find that material.

•

Omi Marta at age fifty-eight with Gabriele at two years old.
Omi Marta looked like this when she came to live with us.

On the other hand, Omi Marta was also very strict, and I had to obey her to the letter and immediately. When her bridge circle met at our house, I was not under any circumstances to make any noise, and I was not to leave anything, toys or books, in her room, nor was I to enter it while visitors were there. I had to be as quiet as a six-year-old can possibly be. When I was not, the punishment was swift and sure.

Omi learned to speak Dutch very quickly and got along famously with all the neighbor children who were my friends, especially Carla, as well as with my friends from school, so that all the other children ended up calling her "Omi" as well. I don't know what she did all day long, as there was little help needed in the household, which, in any event, my mother had well under control. She couldn't have had much contact with her husband, Opa Ernst, in Germany, since the mail between Holland and Germany was disrupted soon after the German army invaded Holland in May of 1940. It cannot have been easy for her or for my mother to share a household, but somehow they did.

It did not seem strange to me that Omi Marta had come to live with us, even though before 1939 our household consisted of only my parents and me. So many things had already changed in my life that even then I knew not to ask any questions, but just to accept that situations had changed.

School

Other than the fact that Omi Marta came to live with us, those early years in Amsterdam were pretty usual for a child. I think my parents rather spoiled me in certain ways. True, I did not get everything I wanted; but I did receive a present on each of my parents' birthdays, and I was convinced that this was absolutely the norm in all families.

In September of 1939 I started the first grade. I don't remember very much of that first school year other than the teacher, the multiplication tables, and learning to read and write. We had the same teacher for the first three grades. I've forgotten her name, but she had brown eyes and brown hair which she wore in a chignon. I though she was very tall. She was also very gentle, and when she had something disagreeable to tell you she would speak to you privately, not in front of the whole class. At the end of the second grade she told me in that manner that I would not be advanced to the third grade but would have to repeat the second.

To learn to write, we wrote on slates first. That was fun; we each had our own slate and, of course, slate-pencils, which we sharpened on the street or on the windowsills. They were very pretty, with colored foil paper around their ends. We kept them in slate-pencil cases, long narrow boxes of light-colored wood with tops that slid open. They were decorated with flowers or fairy tale characters or animals. The other important item was a case shaped like a soft-

Gabriele in December 1940, age 7. This was an official class picture; every child was photographed against this same background, which shows a picture of Sinterklaas and Zwarte Piet.

The leesplankje, *or reading board, with which we learned to read.*

drink can with a cover on each end. It was made of metal and also gaily decorated. We called it a *sponzendoos*, a sponge box, and kept a small, wet sponge in one end and a piece of chamois in the other. Both were necessary to clean our slates.

When we had more or less learned to control our slate pencils, we were allowed to use regular pencils on specially lined paper: two narrow lines together to write the small letters in, and above and below them lines at a greater distance for capital letters. Of course, we didn't "write" immediately. First we drew lines, then lines that hooked downward and that were eventually developed into the letter "i." Finally, after having learned the other letters as well, we practiced with pencils on this lined paper until we made no more mistakes. Then at last we graduated to pen and ink. At the end of the first grade we knew how to write neatly and without blotches.

Reading was taught in the same gradual way with a *leesplankje*, a reading board. It consisted of a terraced board with pictures on each terrace and words underneath the pictures. After we had learned the letters, the teacher gave us cardboard "tiles" with letters on them, and we had to match them to the words beneath the pictures. I still remember the first few words on the board: *Aap, noot, Mies, Wim, zus, Jet*—monkey, nut, Mies (a proper name), Wim (another name), sis (short for sister), and Jet (also a proper name). I loved books; I wanted to read them by myself, so I learned to read very quickly. I loved the idea that now I could read all the books I wanted by myself; I no longer had to wait until somebody had the time and inclination to read to me. From the moment I could read, I became a bookworm!

Opa Ernst in his office.
In the background, just behind his head, there is a
photograph of me at approximately three years old.

Tensions in the House

During the years 1938 and 1939 I began to notice tensions in the house, especially after Omi came to live with us. For one thing, Opa Ernst wasn't with us.

•

Where is Opa Ernst? Why isn't he with us? He and Omi are married, so why didn't he come, too? Is he all alone now? Who takes care of him? He sends me a letter and a present for my birthday, but why doesn't he come to see me? Is he nervous and sad, like Omi?

•

I just couldn't understand it. Opa Ernst was Omi Marta's husband; wasn't he *supposed* to be together with her? He used to take me for walks, used to let me "help" in the factory and play in his office, and now, all of a sudden, he was never there.

For another thing, my mother and my grandmother didn't get along too well together in the same household. Each was used to having her own apartment and to doing the work and the cooking the way she wanted it done. Now there were quarrels in the kitchen, disagreements on who did what when, where and why. There was sometimes too much salt in the dinner and sometimes not enough. Every adult was nervous because of the events in Germany; no one knew what was going to happen or what to expect, and even though I was only six years old, I was old enough to understand that "my" adults were not happy and that my world was changing.

Invasion

During the night between May 9 and May 10, 1940, the German army marched into Holland, and for five days there was fighting. Bombs fell with loud explosions, sirens went off all the time, burning planes fell out of the sky, and even at age six I knew that these events were just not normal. Yet I asked no questions, sensing that they would not be welcome. It was the beginning of my "closing up and turning in."

At the end of May 1940 I had my seventh birthday. Once again, Hitler and his hordes had not given me a very good birthday present! I watched from our third-story window to see soldiers marching through the streets.

·

They sure march funny! What are they doing here? And why does it make everybody so frightened? I don't like the look on Papi's face. And I've never seen Mami cry before. Grownups don't cry! Omi doesn't want to come and look, but you can hear those boots in the whole house anyway. What a horrible sound! Why did they come? They look scary. I don't understand what they want, but I'm scared. I don't like the way they look. I'm frightened; I want to hide.

·

My parents tried to explain "war" to me, but it didn't mean very much to me. Not yet. For the time being, life went on more or less as before. My father continued going to the office; my mother and grandmother continued to run the household; and I continued in school and play.

My Friend Max

Since most homes in Amsterdam were apartments, only the ground-floor residents had small back yards. The other floors had a small balcony, at most. So, as I mentioned earlier, we children played in the street. Carla, the girl from upstairs, Anneke, the girl from the ground-floor apartment, the children of the butcher around the corner, other children, and I played with our dolls, with colorful bouncing balls, or played such other games as the season might dictate. I also had what was called an *autoped*, a scooter with rubber tires around the wheels and handlebars like a bicycle. Going downhill or racing very fast along the street, feeling the wind in my face was one of the most wonderful feelings a child could have. We also had tops shaped like mushrooms, which had to be spun and advanced by a small whip, and that was a favorite game of ours.

I also made friends at school. My best friend from my class was a boy named Max who lived in my street diagonally across from me. We became friends because we were both singled out in class: since neither of us could carry a tune, we were not allowed to sing; but as long as we were quiet we could do whatever we pleased. To this purpose we were made to change seats and occupy a double bench right in front of the teacher. All benches in school were double, but usually the girls sat together and the boys sat together; it was unusual to have a mixed pair. Max and I became fast friends, our parents became acquainted, we played often at each other's houses, and

I can still feel the envy I had one day when Max showed me a pair of *klompen,* Dutch wooden shoes, that he had in his room.

Our friendship finally became really cemented one winter day when Max's father took the two of us skating. Holland's winters are not usually so severe that the canals freeze solid; but that winter, when Max and I were about seven, was very cold and skating was possible on almost every body of water. On that particular day we went skating on a lake, and as the three of us skated toward the edge of the little lake the ice proved to be very thin. It gave way, and all three of us found ourselves in the ice-cold water. But we were lucky: there was a restaurant at the edge of the lake with an outside terrace, and we were able to grasp the edge of the terrace and to hang there, shouting for help, until the restaurant people came and pulled us out. Both mothers were called and came rushing over with dry clothes (the lake was not far from home). Both Max and I were tucked into bed by our respective mothers for the rest of the day, and no harm came to any of us.

My Eighth Birthday

One of my happiest memories of that early war time is that of my eighth birthday.

•

Today is my birthday: I am eight years old. I wake up with a special feeling because today is a very special day. I am allowed to choose which dress I wear to school, and so I choose—somewhat hesitantly—my gray velvet suit. It has a gray velvet skirt that bounces around my legs, a pink blouse with a huge lacy collar, and a gray velvet jacket cut round in front. The collar goes over the jacket, and I feel very dressed up in this dress. I wear pink socks with it and black patent leather shoes. I go to school carrying not only my school bag, but also an enormous paper bag with candy for my class. It's traditional to treat our classmates on our birthdays (we say *trakteren* in Dutch). After that, if we have behaved very nicely in class, we receive permission from the teacher to go to all the other classes to offer candy to their teachers and also perhaps to a special friend in that class. I will make sure that I behave beautifully in class all morning. I may also choose a friend to go with me to all the other classes. Naturally, I choose my girlfriend Peggy. If I am lucky and the other teachers are in a good mood, perhaps they will give me a present—a new notebook or a brand new pencil that doesn't even have its first point yet. I can sharpen it myself.

After school, when I come home, there is a table ready for me with birthday presents on it and, of course, the birthday candles. They are not on a cake; they stand in a blue wooden ring that has pink painted roses on it. It has holes all around for the candles. Today there are eight candles, but there are many holes left over for many more years. In the middle, in the center of the ring between all the other candles, stands one special candle. It's much taller and much thicker than the others. It's white and also has roses on it. It's marked off into twenty-one sections. It's called the "light of life" (*levenslicht* in Dutch), and only the appropriate section is burned. Today I light the candle, but I must blow it out when it reaches section nine—that's for next year. All the other candles will burn down to the end.

On this birthday most of the presents are books; there is a huge stack of them on my table. Many are popular children's books of the day, but many others are books of Greek and Roman myths, books about animals, and other subjects. A friend of my father's, Dr. Kurt Singer, gives me a magic instrument, a kaleidoscope, which fascinates me. I have never seen such a thing, and Dr. Singer has to show me how to use it and what it does. I cannot put it down; the shapes and the colors are so beautiful, and I can imagine so many stories just by looking at them! Dr. Singer visits us often; he makes me laugh because he is much smaller than my father and because he has a mane of snow-white hair which stands around his head like a halo. He is always very nice to me and treats me not like a child, but like any other human being. He never talks down to me.

In the evening, when we finally have dinner, I get my favorite food. I always choose the same thing every year: chicken with rice. For dessert I choose chocolate pudding with vanilla sauce. And for this one day of the year, I don't even have to finish everything on my plate!

On the weekend I have a party for my friends, both those from school and others as well. We eat all sorts of good things. Mami has baked a cheesecake because that is my favorite, and we drink hot chocolate. Then Mami leads us in all sorts of games. One of the most popular games is a German one called *Topfschlagen*, or Beat the Pot. One by one we are blindfolded and turned around several times. We have a wooden spoon, and the pot is somewhere in the room. We must find it, so we crawl around on all fours accompanied by the shouts of the other children: *Warm! Hot! Cold! Warmer! Colder!* depending on whether we get closer to the pot or farther away. Finally we find the pot, and now comes the best part: first we bang on the pot with the wooden spoon as long and hard as we can to make plenty of noise. Everybody cheers. Then we take off the blindfold, beat the pot some more, and finally, with much ceremony and more cheers, we lift the pot and find—a surprise! Every child receives a small present this way, but the best part is the fun!

Eventually everybody goes home and I am sent to bed, exhausted but very happy. Tomorrow I will wear my school clothes again; there will be no more *trakteren*, no more candles or cheesecake or presents for another year. But tonight I go to bed happy.

New Rules

In those first few years of their occupation, the Nazis gave a variety of rules and regulations designed to hinder the Jews in every way possible. Of many I was then unaware, since at my age I didn't read either the daily newspapers or *Het Joodsche Weekblad,* "The Jewish Weekly," which was published by the *Joodsche Raad,* the Jewish Council. Jews were dismissed from their posts in government and public agencies; Jewish physicians could no longer practice; and many other occupations were forbidden to Jews. Property and bank accounts were confiscated, as were bicycles, radios, and all objects made of copper, bronze, nickel, tin, and lead. All jewelry and all gold or silver objects also had to be handed over, and the forced division of the Jewish and non-Jewish populations became ever stricter. Beginning in 1941 Jews were no longer permitted to go to parks, zoos, cafés, swimming pools, or most other public places. Jews were not even permitted to sit on the benches in public parks or on the streets. Posters saying *"Voor Joden verboden,"* "Forbidden to Jews," were displayed everywhere. Also in 1941 the Nazis gave the order that all Jewish children had to go to a Jewish school, and although the law forbidding us to go to concerts and the theater did not affect me directly, this school decree did, of course. Jewish children had to be taught by Jewish teachers and had to be kept separated from non-Jewish children in school as well as out of school. I was lucky; I did not have to change schools as so many others did.

NIEUWE EDITIE: 2e JAARGANG No. 17a · 7 AUGUSTUS 1942 (24 MENACHEM 5702

Het Joodsche Weekblad

UITGAVE VAN DEN JOODSCHEN RAAD VOOR AMSTERDAM

SECRETARIAAT DER REDACTIE
JODEN BREESTRAAT 93
TELEFOON 51736-41828

ADMINISTRATIE EN EXPEDITIE
JOACHIMSTHAL'S
BOEKHANDEL, UITGEVERS
EN DRUKKERIJBEDRIJF N.V.
JODEN BREESTRAAT 93
TELEFOON 44240-44740

onder verantwoordelykheid van A. Asscher en Prof. Dr. D. Cohen

EXTRA EDITIE

De Duitsche autoriteiten maken bekend:

1. Alle Joden, die niet onverwijld gevolg geven aan een tot hen gerichten oproep voor de arbeidsverruiming in Duitschland, worden gevangen genomen en naar het concentratiekamp Mauthausen gebracht.

   Deze of andere straf wordt niet toegepast op die Joden, die zich nog achteraf voor uiterlijk Zondag 9 Augustus 1942, te 5 ure aanmelden, of verklaren, dat zij bereid zijn, aan de werkverruiming deel te nemen.

2. Alle Joden, die geen jodenster dragen, zullen naar het concentratiekamp Mauthausen gebracht worden.

3. Alle Joden, die zonder toestemming der autoriteiten van woonplaats of woning veranderen - ook indien zij dit slechts tijdelijk doen - worden naar het concentratiekamp Mauthausen gebracht.

Page of Het Joodsche Weekblad, The Jewish Weekly, *stating that anyone disobedient to the orders published here will be sent to the concentration camp Mauthausen.*

Voor Joden verboden

DE PROCUREUR-GENERAAL
FUNG. GEWESTELIJK DIRECTEUR VAN POLITIE

FEITSMA

C 377

The "Forbidden to Jews" poster,
which appeard in shop windows in Holland.

The school on Jekerstraat (Jeker Street) that I attended was designated a Jewish school. But my non-Jewish schoolmates had to leave, and other "new" children came in. It made us feel insecure; what happened to our friends could just as easily happen to us. I did not talk to my friends about this, and in any event, my non-Jewish friends disappeared from one day to the next. It made me think, though.

•

Where did they go? There are so many schools here, how did they know which school to go to? Or were they told that as well? Will I ever see them again? I don't understand. We always played together; why can't we just go on as before? It doesn't make sense—they are still the same and I am still the same, but now the Nazis say that we are not the same. Can I disappear like that? I guess so. If they can, then I can too. Where would I be if I disappeared?

•

Many other things changed as well. One of the new regulations was that Jews could no longer shop for food or other goods when or where they wanted. We could only go to those stores which did not have the "Forbidden to Jews" poster in the window, and then only between 3:00 and 5:00 P.M. That affected me directly, because it made it difficult, if not impossible, for me to run errands for my mother, which I had always loved to do. But school let out at 4:00 in the afternoon, and that didn't leave much time for me to run any errands. We were not allowed to have certain items at all, such as fruit or milk. Of course, shopping so late in the afternoon also ensured that Jews did not find the best quality goods, which of course had been sold first. Some bakers and grocers, though, who were sympathetic to us and hated the occupation would keep things in the back room for us, and when we came in would sell us fresh vegetables, bread, and other staples against the rules and orders of the Nazis, thereby risking severe punishment.

Not only were we no longer allowed to associate with non-Jews, we also had to be home—in our own homes, not just indoors—at 8:00 P.M. Then there was a curfew until 6:00 the next morning. The ban on our associations meant that I could no longer play with Carla and others in the street. I wasn't really concerned with the curfew, though, for 8:00 P.M. was my bedtime anyway.

Non-Jews were not permitted to shop for Jews, either, but where we lived we were able to circumvent both the shopping restrictions and the non-association order easily. The entrance to our apartment had one flight of stairs leading to the apartment proper; Carla's family's apartment on the fourth floor had two. Inside the apartments, their apartment had one flight of stairs to the attic, whereas ours had two. Thus the attics of the two apartments were on the same level, and they were connected by a narrow door. Carla's mother, whom I called Tante Trien, Aunt Trien, was therefore able to give my mother the things she had bought for us, and Carla and I were able to go to each other's houses to play—all without public exposure. I was not aware then that there was considerable danger in all this. Had the Nazis found us out, it would at the very least have meant deportation for Carla's family as well as ours. It was all very confusing for a child, and although Carla and I discussed it all many times, we both remained confused, and I was very frightened. There were so many things to remember; every day there were new things that had been allowed and were now no longer allowed because I was a Jew. And I wasn't even really sure what "being a Jew" meant!

I'm sure my parents tried to shelter me from many things, but it was inevitable that their nervousness and anxiety seeped through and that I felt them.

The Yellow Star

On April 29, 1942,[1] the order was made public that all Jews had to wear a distinguishing mark: a yellow Star of David with a black outline, as big as the palm of a man's hand, with the word "Jew" written in the middle in black, vaguely Hebrew-shaped letters. The order went into effect on May 2. Everyone six years old and older had to wear the star on all outer clothing, on the left side over the heart. The star had to be sewn on very firmly all around the edges; we were not allowed to pin it on or to sew it just at the corners.

•

My father sits me down:

Now, this is a Star of David. The Nazis have said that we Jews have to wear this star all the time. You must be very proud of this star, just as proud as the Catholics are of the cross. It is a badge of pride for us.

There are several problems with that little speech, however.

Who is David? Why David, why not Fritz, Papi's name? Why does it have a black edge? I know that envelopes and letters have black edges when somebody has died. Does this black edge mean the same? Are we going to die if we wear that star? Why is it yellow? And the letters look funny; they wiggle. At school, teacher says that I mustn't wiggle my letters! What is a Jew, anyway? They keep saying Jews may not do things. I don't know what a Jew is. I guess it makes us different, but I don't think we are different from how we were before. And why am I supposed to be proud? Papi never said that before. Nobody ever said that!

The yellow Star of David, also known as the "Jewish Star,"
which every Jew from six years old onward had to wear,
with the word "Jew" in Dutch.

Many Dutch people were as angry as the Jews themselves about this forced division of marked and unmarked people. Their anger showed in a solidarity with us. One day, while I was playing in the street, I saw a man pass with a bright yellow star attached to the lapel of his coat. Made of paper, it was held on by two safety pins. I don't remember what was written on it, but many Dutch in those first days wore yellow flowers as a sign of solidarity with us, or even a Star of David cut out of yellow paper with the words "Jew and non-Jew are *one*" written inside.

As I mentioned before, we were a totally assimilated family, as my grandparents also had been, and as such we had never gone to synagogue or kept Jewish holidays or customs. Therefore there was no answer to my questions about what it meant to be a Jew or why I was to be proud of it. Still, I mouthed those words whenever I felt it was appropriate. Among the people I told about my father's conversation with me was Tante Trien, Carla's mother. She was so pleased with what I said that she told me to come up to their apartment every morning before school and she would give me some sweets. Naturally, that pleased me no end!

Unusual Lessons

From now on we begin each school day with some very different lessons. Every morning the teacher looks to see whether all of us are present, and we also look. As of 1941 Jews have been sent to "work camps," and since January 1942 groups of Jews have been deported to Westerbork, a concentration camp in the province of Drenthe. Other people have gone into hiding—what we call *onderduiken*, to dive under. If any child is missing from class, the teacher sends a friend of that child to his or her house to find out what has happened.

The day comes when this happens to me. Peggy, my girlfriend, is absent, and the teacher sends me to find out why. Now, this is not such an easy task. School starts at nine o'clock, and any adult who sees a child on the streets after that time can—and does—stop that child and ask all sorts of questions as to why that child is not in school. In addition, German soldiers roam the streets and can stop a person and ask questions. So when I am sent to Peggy's house, I try to be as inconspicuous as possible, particularly where the soldiers are concerned. I go to Peggy's house, where she lives with her aunt and uncle, ring the bell, and when no one answers, ring it again and again and again. Finally a neighbor comes out and asks me what I want.

What do you want? And why aren't you in school? It's after nine o'clock.

Please, Mevrouw, Ma'am, my teacher sent me to find out where Peggy is. She is not in class. But no one answers the doorbell. Isn't anyone home? Do you know anything?

Yes, the neighbor tells me, *they are gone. They've been taken away.*

Although I know this can happen, it is still very frightening to have it happen to such a close friend. Not only is it a big loss, it leaves an empty space and makes me wonder who will be next and what will happen to my family and me.

It is my second big loss. My friend Max has also disappeared, and I don't know what happened to him and his family either. He disappeared in 1942, and it will not be until 1987 that Max "re-discovers" me and we each find out what happened to the other.

After the roll call the teacher checks to see that we're all wearing our stars. Occasionally one of us does not have one, and in that case someone else must lend the starless child a jacket or a sweater with a star so that in case of an inspection we will all be wearing stars as ordered.

Then comes the first lesson of the day. The teacher asks us, *What will you say if a soldier comes into our class and asks you how the fruit tasted last night?*

We have to be sure to give the "correct" answer: *We did not have any fruit. We are not allowed to buy any.*

Another favorite question is: *What time did your parents come home?*

Whatever we answer to that, it has to be before the curfew hour, but not too close to it or exactly 8:00 P.M.. It has to sound natural.

There are other questions of the same kind concerning forbidden food or forbidden places. The teacher varies the questions from day to day. Of course, we may very well have had fruit; our parents may have managed to come home after 8:00 P.M.; but we are never to reveal that. It is perhaps the only time we are taught as a school lesson to lie convincingly. Our lives depend on it, and we know it. Not only that, but we have to keep apart what we are taught at home and at school. At home my parents have taught me that lying is bad; at school the teacher teaches me that lying is essential. Somehow the two lessons do not interfere with each other, and I am able to keep the two types of lying separate. Yet that too is confusing and frightening.

I know I have to tell the truth at home. But I have to lie to the "Moffen" (the Germans). One is bad; the other is good. How do I know which is which? How can I remember? Grownups are so confusing: they say one thing one day and the opposite the next day. And if I don't keep it straight, I'll get punished. Maybe the Moffen will send me away like Peggy. Or they'll send Mami and Papi and Omi away. It's all very difficult.

Somehow I learn to accept that both sets of adults can be right, even though they say opposite things. I have to accept the contradiction and just do the best I can with it.

The Sandals and Other Worries

I have smaller worries, too. My mother comes home one day with a surprise for me.

Here, this is for you!

What is it, Mami, what is it? Oh, it's heavy!

Mami helps me to open the package; I am impatient and cut the string. It's a pair of sandals, just like all the girls are wearing and I've been wanting for a long time: wooden soles to make lots of noise with and leather straps to hold them on. I take one look at them and cry:

I can't wear these, Mami!

Why not?

Because they're red and black!

My mother insists that I try them on, and they fit beautifully.

But I still can't wear them; I can't go to school with something in red and black.

Mami still doesn't understand. Yet to me it's so logical.

Mami, red and black are the colors of the NSB (Nationaal Socialistische Beweging—the Dutch Nazi party). *Everyone knows that! I'm Jewish, you said so. I can't wear those colors!*

In the end I throw a tantrum. I cry and scream until Mami finally promises to have the black straps changed to blue, then I proudly clatter around in my wooden sandals.

On the way to or from school I often have to wait for long lines of army trucks to pass before I can cross the street—another frightening experience. No soldier ever speaks to me on these occasions, but I am always afraid that one may.

What will I say? I don't know how to talk to him. I don't know what to call him. I can't just call him "Mof." You can only call them that behind their backs. If he talks to me, does that mean he will take me away? If he does, will Mami and Papi know what happened to me? Where I have disappeared to? Do I show that I speak German or pretend that I speak only Dutch?

It also occurs to me that I might return home after school some day and not find anybody there, that during school time soldiers might have come to take my parents and grandmother away.

Then what will I do? What will happen to me? Do I go to Tante Trien? But that's dangerous for them. But I can't just live alone!

•

Those were questions without answers; at nine years old I couldn't possibly have answered them, at least not in theory. Had any of these things actually happened, I might have been able to survive on my own; certainly other children did. But as it turned out, those things never happened. Still, these questions remained shadows in my mind and made me uncomfortable and scared. Yet I never shared these anxieties, either with my parents and Omi or with my friends. Instead I became more closed up and turned in. I took my clues from the adults around me; they explained to me only what was strictly necessary (or what they considered strictly necessary) and never talked about the war when I was present. So I, in my turn, did not tell them about my concerns. It was an upside-down world where my "mighty" grownups were as afraid, nervous and helpless as I, a child, was.

Black-Outs and Window Tapes

There were other anxieties too. All our windows had to be totally blacked out, with not a thread of light showing anywhere. My father came home one day with rolls of pitch-black paper, which he fashioned into window shades. These he hung in front of the windows to make blinds, which we pulled down every evening before we turned on the lights. When the lights were turned off, the rooms were impenetrably black. I was afraid ever after that maybe, just maybe, a tiny shred of light would show through or that the paper might tear, and then who knew what would happen? It was just one more thing to be afraid of.

•

I am not a particularly courageous child, but I am not fearful, either. Now, though, I begin to be afraid of the dark, begin to wonder what might be happening in such dark surroundings and who might be hidden there. I do not sleep with a night light, but I begin having a recurrent dream in which a huge Junebug comes into my room and sets my bed afire, beginning at the right corner of the foot of the bed. The flames are very slow and very bright blue and orange in color. I never dream this dream all the way to the end; I am never burnt in it, but it frightens me enormously. Yet this, too, I do not tell my parents or Omi, nor do I go to seek solace with anyone else. I feel that it is wiser to keep silent, even though it is also more frightening. But it "wouldn't do" to upset my parents or grandmother. They already have enough worries.

In addition to the black-out, another order is published and one day I find my parents busy putting brown packing tape on the windows, the bands of tape crisscrossing the glass in a star pattern.

Mami, what is that?

It's packing tape.

But you aren't packing anything!

No, we have to put it on the windows.

But…you can't pack the windows, can you?

No, of course not. We leave the windows where they are, but we have to put the sticky tape on it.

Why?

So that they won't shatter.

Why would they shatter? They never have before.

They might shatter if a bomb falls close to the house.

What does a bomb have to do with our windows?

When a bomb falls, it pushes air aside, and then that air can push on the window glass. If it pushes too hard the glass breaks. We don't want pieces of glass all over the floor, and we don't want a piece to cut us if we happen to be close to the window when it breaks.

Why would a bomb fall in our street?

Well, Papi explained to you what war is, remember? In a war bombs get thrown out of airplanes, and sometimes they fall in places where they're not really supposed to fall.

Why?

At this point my mother has had enough of my questions, and ends the conversation in her usual manner:

Lirum, Larum, Loeffelstiel; kleine Kinder fragen viel, which means something like *Crickety, crackety, cooking pot; little children ask a lot,* a formula used by many mothers to express something like *My word, but you are asking a lot of questions again!*

So I keep my questions to myself, even though all this doesn't make much sense, and just watch as Mami and Omi finish putting sticky tape on every window in the house.

•

Eventually a bomb did indeed fall in the street on our block, though at the other end of the block from our house. And the windows did indeed break—that is, the windows of all the houses except ours. Whether that was due to our "superior" manner of taping the windows or just because the bomb fell too far away to have any effect on our windows, I didn't know then and don't know now. But I did learn the connection between bombs and windows.

There was always a lot of uncertainty: would a bomb fall? Would the city be bombed? Would a plane crash in our street? Would anyone see light glimmering though the black blinds? What would happen next? Would the air raid siren go off? An air raid siren had been installed on the roof, and any time it went off we had to hide in a shelter. It was very loud, and when all was quiet during the night it sounded even louder. I found it very frightening. Everyone was helpless in these circumstances, and I, a child, even more so. Again I didn't say anything, but I felt it in the house and among other adults.

I had always liked to read; now I began to read even more. The stories in the books were so much more pleasant, so much more equanimous than real life. The adventures of mythological gods and heroes and the adventures of Harlekijntje (Little Harlequin, a series of Dutch children's books) or of a little girl called Nesthaeckchen in German or Benjaminnetje in Dutch (the Benjamin, or youngest, of the family) were so much more ordinary than my own life. I also began to tell myself stories, both fairy tales and other fantasies. All of it was more ordinary than the real world. The real world was far too bizarre and uncertain. I did not dare look it directly in the face.

The *Knijpkat*

In order to be able to walk through the house when all was blacked
out at night, and after the light had been turned off, or to find our
way inside an air raid shelter, we had a number of flashlights in the
house. These were no ordinary flashlights with batteries. A battery
might not work, or it might fall out; there were many other objec-
tions. No, these were very special flashlights. In Dutch they were
called *knijpkat*, literally "squeeze-cat." In order to keep the light going you had to keep squeezing the handle, the "tail" of the cat.
When you squeezed, which you had to do very, very quickly to get
light, the flashlight made a noise like a purring cat. According to the
dictionary, this kind of flashlight is called a dyno-torch, but I've
never heard that term or seen a flashlight like that since the war.
There is a small dynamo in the flashlight which keeps the light
shining, much like the dynamo mounted on a bicycle wheel that is
kept going by the turning of the wheel. We had one *knijpkat* for
each person in the household, and I was fascinated by them. Later
we took them with us to the concentration camps and brought at
least one of them back home again, which I still have to this day. I
don't remember ever having to use it, but I was very glad to have
one of my own.

Pick-Ups

After October 1942 the Nazis come more often to pick up Jews from their houses (*oppakken*, as we called it), rather than notify them to assemble at a given point. Their measures become stricter, as the Nazis want to be sure to have a certain number of Jews leaving the country, to be "relocated" at any given time.

One night my mother comes into my room very late, about midnight, wakes me up and tells me:

Get dressed very quickly. We are going out.

Why? Where are we going?

You'll see. No questions, now; get ready very quickly. Hurry!

We emerge from the apartment into the dark, silent streets where any noise means danger and where we have to hide quickly whenever we hear other footsteps.

Where are we going? Why don't they tell me? I'm not going to say anything. I'm a big girl already. I can run fast; they won't catch us because of me. I wish I knew what's going on.

We walk for what seems like a very long time. After maybe forty-five minutes we end up in a place, a restaurant perhaps, where Omi Marta is employed as a potato peeler. People who peel potatoes are on a "safe" list; they will not be deported. There are a number of "safe" occupations; my mother is registered as a "fur worker" for list purposes. These lists supposedly prevent one from being deported, but usually they are declared invalid after a while.

This night all four of us peel potatoes. I sit on a low stool all night long. Someone has given me a knife, and I peel potatoes as best I can. I am nine years old, and I know very well that our lives depend on those potato peels.

I have to do this right, not take off too much potato with the peel. If I do it wrong, if I make a mistake, they'll come and they'll find us and they'll take us away. All of us, all four of us.

We return home the next morning, but the shock of being awakened and having to run away in the middle of the night, defying the curfew, remains.

Another night I suddenly wake up when somebody turns on the light in my room. Again I am told to dress quickly. When I come into the living room a member of the "Zwarte" stands in the middle of the room. The Dutch police were called "Zwarte," the black police, because of the color of their uniforms. The Zwarte has come to pick us up, and so, once again in the middle of the night, we have to go to the Hollandsche Schouwburg, the Dutch National Theater, which is one of Amsterdam's theaters and also, in these times, the place where Jews are collected before deportation. Because of this it acquires the nickname "Joodsche Schouwburg," Jewish Theater, in 1941.

When we get to the Schouwburg, Mami makes me lie down on a red cot and tells me to go to sleep. The cot is too short even for me, who am small for my age, and I am unable to sleep because again I have no idea what is going to happen next. Also there are a great many people in the Schouwburg, and there is an atmosphere of surprise and discomfort mixed with panic. People are trying to find others they know, trying to keep calm, trying to keep their children calm, trying to find somebody—anybody—to help them. Women cry, men shout, children wail or run about. People are called out of the room and come back in; new arrivals try to find a place; papers are asked for and given back; nobody really knows anything, and none of anyone's questions are answered. Chaos reigns. Slowly the night passes, and when dawn breaks the real surprise is that the Nazis let us leave to go home.

In between these trips I have to continue school, of course. "Continue" is perhaps not the best word; too many children disappear from one day to the next, and we never know whether our teacher will still be the same the next day. Just as I get used to one teacher, she disappears and another one takes over. Then the process of acclimatization has to start all over again, only to have the new teacher disappear as well. Being by nature a very shy child, it is a very difficult situation for me. The more children disappear and the more teachers change, the more anxious I become over leaving home every day.

Is anybody going to be there when I come home from school? Will the apartment be empty? Will I be able to get in, or will the door be sealed? What am I going to do? I wish I could see into the apartment before I ring the bell. I wish I knew what's going to happen next.

At home, meanwhile, we have prepared everything for having to leave on short, if any, notice. "Everything" consists of one rucksack per person (with a smaller one for me), for clothing and a rolled-up blanket tied to the outside, and one "breadsack" per person for food. (A breadsack looked somewhat like today's sports bags and was carried diagonally over one shoulder, the strap crossing the chest.) As well, several layers of clothing lie ready for us to put on, so that we will have not only the clothes in the rucksack but also whatever we wear. My doll Peter is ready as well, dressed in his green three-piece outfit.

•

Actually, my teddy bear Brunette was my favorite toy. She was named after the baby bear in the story "Goldilocks," in the Dutch version of which all three bears have names. She had become an extension of myself, a sister, perhaps, and certainly my confidante to whom I told all my joys and woes, from learning to read (which made me ecstatic) to being teased by other children (which made

My beloved bear, Brunette.

me both sad and angry), to my fears about the Nazis. She was more than a mere toy; to me she was a real person. That she never actually responded made no difference at all, because in my mind she did respond. Because of these feelings I did not want to take her; the uncertainty over where we would be going was such that I did not want to expose Brunette to whatever it was that would happen to us.

•

Brunette, therefore, goes to "dive under"—she goes into hiding. She moves upstairs to Carla's house and care.

If Brunette is in a safe place, then I am too, kind of, and nothing really bad can happen to me, because nothing really bad will happen to her. Carla will keep her, and she will take good care of her when I have to go away. Brunette will be all right with Carla. Then, when we come back, she'll come back to me and we'll be together again.

At the same time, Carla and I make another arrangement against the day when we will be picked up.

Carla, listen up a minute. Look, I've written you a note telling you that we've been picked up and that you shouldn't ring our doorbell or come to the apartment through the attic. 'Cause it would be dangerous for you. I don't know when they'll come for us. It could be in the night, like before. Then I won't be able to call you or anything. So I'll leave this note in your mail box, okay? That way you'll know.

We are both nine years old.

Deportation

The day on which I leave my carefully prepared note is Sunday, June 20, 1943, and I have been ten years old for three weeks. It's a blisteringly hot day on which the Nazis conduct round-the-clock *razzias*, roundups, in East and South Amsterdam. Our apartment is in South Amsterdam. That day 5,500 Jews are taken and deported, among whom is my family: my father, my mother, my grandmother, and I. The "Groene," the "green police," who are Nazi soldiers wearing green uniforms, come at about nine or ten o'clock in the morning, ring the doorbell, bang on the door, and order us in loud, harsh voices to hurry, hurry: "*Schnell, schnell! 'raus, 'raus,*" get out, get out.

Everything has to be done in a hurry. Nevertheless, after going downstairs I hang back and manage to slip the note to Carla through the letter box in the front door. (Ironically, she never got it, for her mother found it before she did and decided that the news would be too hard on Carla. As a result, one of the first questions Carla asked me after our return two years later was "Why didn't you leave me the note you promised me?" When I explained that I had indeed left the note, the whole story came out.)

On our arrival in the street we find all the neighbors there, many of them crying, others trying to give us last-minute things to take along such as small food items. Mevrouw Gijtenbeek, who manages the corner grocery store, Van Amerongen, and who knows all the neighborhood children by name, can't stop crying long enough to give me a small bag of sweets she has brought for me—my favorite kind. All she can do is just put it in my hand, embrace me tightly, and hold me for a minute.

The Groene tells us to hurry, then to wait, to wait some more, and then some more. Finally an army truck arrives. We call these trucks *overvalwagen* in Dutch, army assault trucks. They have a cab in front and an open back which can be—and on this day is—covered with a canvas "roof." There are no benches or seats, and it is dark inside. The soldiers order us in, again "*Schnell, schnell!*" "Rush! Rush!" My parents lift me in first and I make my way to the front of the truck, next to the cab, and sit down on my rucksack. I have hardly done so when a large fat woman sits down on top of me, hiding me totally.

Hey! Hey! I'm here too! You're sitting on me! You're hiding me! Get off me! I can't breathe!

She doesn't hear me. I try to push her off, but she is far too heavy, and I am not strong enough to push her away. At last I burst into tears, and my parents hear me, see what has happened, and ask the woman to get off. She has not even realized that she is sitting on me, and she never does apologize!

The assault truck takes us to the Daniel Willinkplein, one of the big squares in Amsterdam and the only one at that time with a "skyscraper"—all of eleven stories high. (After the war the square was renamed Victorieplein, or Victory Square.) Here we get out of the truck and sit down in the street on the sidewalk to wait. Under that blazing hot sun and in our many layers of clothing, it does not take long for us to become overheated. I am wearing two or three layers plus a heavy *loden* coat and a pair of high lace-up boots that I "inherited" from my cousin Werner, and I feel like I'm being baked. Yet the waiting goes on and on. Finally, toward mid-afternoon, the Nazis order us back into the assault truck and we ride off to the

Centraal Station, the Central Railway Station of Amsterdam.

Trains consisting of cattle cars stand waiting. We are pushed in, ordered again to do everything "*schnell, schnell,*" the doors are closed tightly and the train begins to move. For some reason the doors of our car are not tightly closed, and my father pushes me in front of the narrow opening so that I can get some air. I do not think of anything at all during that journey, I do not feel afraid, I do not ask questions or say anything. From that moment on my thinking and feeling systems are completely closed down. The cattle car door might be open, but my door to me has been slammed shut. I simply move my body, but a part of me has been left behind with Brunette—*ondergedoken,* as the Dutch say, dived under, submerged; but during the war it has the special meaning of "in hiding."

•

I don't remember exactly how long this hellish journey lasted, but it was dark when we arrived in Westerbork. Since it was summer and darkness did not fall until ten or eleven o'clock at night, it was a journey of at least eight hours. To go from Amsterdam to Westerbork today takes barely two hours.

Westerbork

JUNE 20, 1943–JANUARY 18, 1944

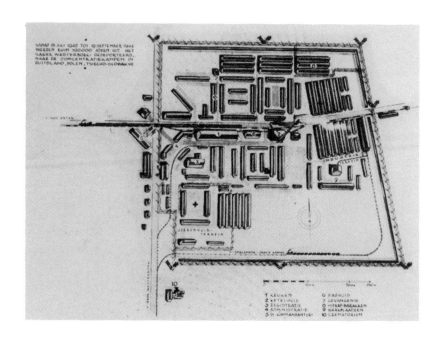

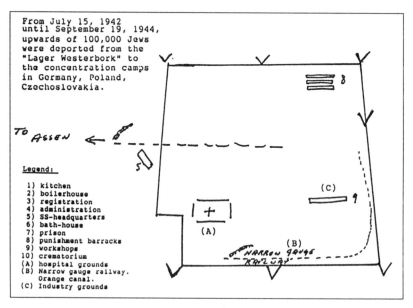

From July 15, 1942
until September 19, 1944,
upwards of 100,000 Jews
were deported from the
"Lager Westerbork" to
the concentration camps
in Germany, Poland,
Czechoslovakia.

TO ASSEN

Legend:

1) kitchen
2) boilerhouse
3) registration
4) administration
5) SS-headquarters
6) bath-house
7) prison
8) punishment barracks
9) workshops
10) crematorium
(A) hospital grounds
(B) Narrow gauge railway.
    Orange canal.
(C) Industry grounds

Schematic plan of Concentration Camp Westerbork.
My drawing (below) follows this outline and gives the legend at the bottom
as well as the remark on the left side of the photo.

Arrival in the Camp and the Barracks

The train stops. The doors are yanked open noisily, and we are all ordered out. We blink in the searchlights, trying to see where we are, what this place is, where we are to go. All is confusion. We cannot really see beyond the searchlights, but what we can see is gray-black, dusty, and full of moving shadows. The big wood-and-barbed-wire gate opens, and we enter this strange, threatening land. None of us knows where we're going. The people in front of us stumble; the people behind us push; the Nazis shout; we hear clicking sounds coming from what looks like a building. Clicking? Typewriters? Here, in this place?

Yes, indeed. The building turns out to be a wooden barracks, furnished with long tables on which stand the typewriters we hear. We are made to go through this barracks in order to "register." The long line of people slowly snakes into the interior of this extraordinary "office." Somehow, somewhere, my mother finds a chair for me and tells me to wait outside.

Now, you sit here and wait for us. Don't go away; just wait patiently until we return. We'll come back for you when we have registered. Be a good girl, now.

And off she goes, back into line with my father and grandmother. The line shuffles forward interminably as each person in turn

The "registration office" in Concentration Camp Westerbork,
through which we had to pass on arrival.

disappears into the barracks. Strangely, I see nobody come out. At ten years old, I consider myself a big girl, practically an adult, but these disappearances worry me.

Where are they going? What are they doing? Why do they have to go there? What's happening to them? Why wasn't I allowed to go with Mami, Papi, and Omi? What if they don't come back for me? Are they going to come back for me? Are they ever going to come back? Maybe I'll never see them again. Everybody just disappears. I don't like this. It's dark here. I'm scared. This chair is hard, I'm uncomfortable, I have to go to the bathroom. Where is everybody? Why is no one coming out? Maaami! Maaamiii, where are you? I want my mami! Mami, don't leave me!

By this time big tears are rolling down my face. I'm sobbing and hiccupping at the same time, I'm terrified, I don't know what to do and no one is there to help me. I feel abandoned and totally helpless.

Eventually, after what seems like hours, some adult sees me, listens to my troubled tale, and goes to find my mother. She makes her way out of the barracks, comes back to me, takes me by the hand and leads me into the barracks.

Why are you crying? Why are you so upset? Didn't I tell you we would come back for you?

Yes, you did; but nobody came out of that barracks and I thought maybe you would also never come back out again, either, and I would never see you again.

After the "registration" comes the "medical examination," for which we have to strip naked. We are also "deloused," although we don't have any lice, and finally we are assigned to a barracks. Ours is Number 65: a long, low, wooden building, as most of the buildings are in Westerbork, with an entrance in the middle of the long side of the barracks leading to a sort of short hallway. These large barracks measure about 280 feet in length by about 32 feet in width by about 18 feet in height.[2] Inside are two enormous rooms, one on either side of the hallway. In Number 65 the room on the right side is for the men and boys over eight years old; the left side is for the women and children, including boys under eight. Each room houses about three hundred people in three-tiered metal bunk beds. One row of these stands against each outside wall, a double row stands in the middle of the room. Two sets of these three-tiered bunk beds are pushed together. In the narrow space between each set of two beds there is a wooden table with two backless wooden benches. In Number 65 there is also a very small black stove, to be stoked with wood. On each of the short ends of the barracks is a washroom, one for all the men, the other for all the women. Long sinks run along the middle of the washroom with cold water faucets about every three feet. There is no warm or hot water. In one corner of each washroom is one toilet, to be used by all the women or men, as the case might be. In some of the barracks these are flush toilets, although mostly these don't work. In most barracks they are chemical toilets (as we call them today).

The beds have straw sacks for mattresses, but we have brought our own blankets. The beds are already occupied when we arrive, as we find out when we sit on them. The original occupants are fleas,

One of the big rooms in the barracks in Westerbork, with its bunk beds. The straw-sack mattresses and pillows can be clearly seen.

Toilet in one of the big barracks' washrooms in Westerbork.

and they are not happy that we are invading their territory. Mami, Omi, and I share two beds on a middle level; it is common to share beds this way, as there are many more people than beds.

Even today I can see as clearly as in 1943 my mother kneeling on the bed in Westerbork going after fleas in a blanket with a pair of scissors. She tries to cut them in half, but doesn't succeed too well; she has not yet learned to catch them with her fingers and kill them with her nails (and where, indeed, would she have acquired such a skill?). In a short space of time, however, we all learn to catch and kill them, and I in particular become an expert flea catcher and killer.

These beds are not only our beds; they are also our closets, chairs, and everything else we need. There are no curtains or any other kind of partition between the beds, so we have no privacy at all. Nor do we have any personal space in which to store our clothing or other belongings, so everything stays on the bed or under the mattress. My doll Peter therefore sits on our bed during the day—until the day I return to the barracks and discover that someone has played with him or used him in some way and has damaged his head. From then on I carry him with me wherever I go, talk to him and confide to him what I cannot talk about with anyone else. He never takes Brunette's place entirely—she is very special; but I love Peter dearly.

Westerbork:
Location and Description

Westerbork is located in the province of Drenthe (also spelled Drente), not far from the city of Assen in the Dutch countryside about eighty miles east of Amsterdam. There are only small villages around Westerbork; in actual fact, it is in the middle of nowhere. It is a desolate area of heath and fengrounds, boggy and marshy. Because of this, and because of Holland's generally maritime climate, the area is very humid. Clouds of insects are always around, and in the summer the flies are a veritable plague. The wind blows all year round, blowing dust, dirt, and sand from the surrounding heath over and into everything, so that the camp and inmates were painted in shades of gray and black.

The camp was five hundred meters square (i.e., 0.31 square miles), with a total area of twenty-five hectares, or just under sixty-two acres. There were no paved streets or any other paved areas in the camp, so when it rained, which it does very often in Holland, the ground turned into pools of mud which literally sucked our *klompen*, our wooden clogs which we were given to replace our shoes when we arrived, off our feet.

Westerbork was not originally built as a concentration camp. It had been built by the Dutch in 1939 to provide temporary housing to refugees arriving from Germany. It was not until July 1, 1942, that the Nazis took over the camp, renaming it Polizeiliches Durchgangslager Westerbork—Police Transit Camp Westerbork. A

The location of Concentration Camp Westerbork in the middle of nowhere. The barbed wire encircling the camp can be clearly seen. In the background stands one of the seven watchtowers which surrounded the camp.

One of the watchtowers at Concentration Camp Westerbork.

barbed-wire fence almost seven feet high was constructed around the camp's perimeter, with seven watch towers spaced evenly around it. The Nazi guards in those towers made sure that no one tried to escape.

In addition to the large barracks described earlier, there were also some small houses, originally meant for families. Later several families lived in each room of these houses, so they had no privacy either. In addition to having no privacy and no personal space, we had no time to ourselves. We were constantly surrounded by people, and it was always very noisy. Any small thing was reason enough for a quarrel; people were always fighting for space on or near the single small stove. As well, stealing—we called it "organizing"—was an everyday occurrence.

There was no special place for us children at Westerbork—no school, no activities. We were always in somebody's way, always in the wrong place at the wrong time, and consequently everybody yelled at us. Worst of all, the people we loved—family members, teachers, and friends—disappeared from one day to the next.

Next to our Barracks 65 there was a *Strafbaracke*—German for punishment barracks—also called *S-Baracke* for short. This was Barracks 67. It was surrounded by barbed wire: a prison within a prison. Of course, everybody had to work in Westerbork, but the inmates of the S-barracks had to work extra hard, under the supervision of Nazis armed with whips. They wore the blue-and-white striped uniform which prisoners in some of the other camps were also forced to wear, whereas we "regular" inmates wore our own clothes.

During the second week in October 1942, Albert Konrad Gemmeker became the commandant of Westerbork. He wore the green uniform, high boots, and gloves, carried a gun on his hip and a riding crop in his hand, which he frequently beat against his boots. Wherever he went he was accompanied by his German shepherd dog.

Between July 15, 1942, two weeks after the Nazi takeover of

A group of Nazis in Camp Westerbork. Third from left is the commandant, Albert Konrad Gemmeker. His uniform, with the high boots, can be seen in the photo, as can his dog (at left), which always accompanied him.

Westerbork, and September 19, 1944, 104,000 of Holland's 140,000 Jews were deported to Westerbork and thence to Auschwitz, Bergen-Belsen, Sobibor, Theresienstadt (also known as Terezín), and other places.

On April 7 and 8, 1945 the Nazis started to leave Westerbork because the Allies (specifically the Canadians) were approaching. On April 12, 1945, Gemmeker left the camp. That same day, shortly after Gemmeker's departure, the Canadians rode into Westerbork, liberating the 909 Jews still there. All of Holland was liberated by May 5, 1945.

Concentration Camp Westerbork is no more. The barracks have been torn down; today there is a museum before one reaches the former camp terrain. Within the former perimeter of the camp there is now a memorial formed from the railroad rails that ran

The first memorial on the camp terrain of what used to be
Concentration Camp Westerbork: the rails of the
original railway, bent up, rusty, and nicked.

through the middle of the camp. There is also a scale model of the camp, and there is another memorial on the former *Appellplatz*, the place where roll call took place. It consists of white stones inset with gray stones in the shape of a map of Holland. Inset in both types of stones are red bricks, one for each of the 102,000 inmates who died either in Westerbork itself or at one of the other camps to which they were further deported and at which they were murdered. The red bricks set together look like graves.

The second memorial, which was finished in 1992.
It is on what used to be the Appellplatz, or place for roll call on the
original camp terrain. On top of the red bricks are small signs to indicate
who is memorialized: a star for Jews, a flame for Gypsies.
Bricks without signs memorialize resistance fighters.

The plaque near this memorial reads:
"Appelplace. The 102,000 stones symbolize the camp inmates who stood
here for roll call and who were murdered in the concentration and death
camps of Eastern Europe. The stones lying down [colored gray] have
been placed in the form of a map of Holland.
Other than the Jews, about 200 Gypsies and an unknown number
of resistance fighters perished."

Work and Food

Everyone except the children has to work. My father works in the "metal industry." He, who has never been used to hard physical labor, now has to flatten huge metal pipes with an enormous sledgehammer. He wears blue overalls, rather oily, over his clothes and the ubiquitous *klompen* on his feet. My mother also wears different clothes now: she wears a dark-blue training suit (today's sweat suit), and a scarf over her hair. Like my father, she wears *klompen*. Her task is to look after the children of other women who have jobs somewhere in the camp. The children are approximately between the ages of two and eight years, so she is a sort of kindergarten teacher *cum* nursemaid. It is a difficult task, as there is nothing with which to keep the children busy and also because she doesn't know the Dutch children's songs and games. Of course there are no books or coloring books or toys. Even had there been books or toys, they would have been of little use because of the disparate ages of the children. My mother, being tone-deaf and unmusical, cannot even sing to the children. In addition to all that, many children, even the older ones, regress and begin again soiling their clothes and their beds. My mother's job is thus not an easy one.

I, too, at the age of ten, regress and begin wetting the bed again. Not only is that unpleasant for my mother, but also for the lady who sleeps in the bed below mine. Straw sacks do not absorb liquid at all, and my neighbor below does not appreciate the nightly shower.

What work does my grandmother do? Once again she is involved in peeling potatoes, perhaps for the camp kitchen.

As a child of ten, I have no job in Westerbork.

In each barracks certain inmates are designated to go and fetch the food from the kitchen. They bring it to the barracks on small carts and dole it out to the rest of us. There is something called potato soup, though I never see a potato in it. We receive a certain amount of bread each day—not very much, just a few grams per person. It is somewhat gray in color and has an indentation or separation on top. On each portion, in this indentation, a tiny piece of *sana* is stuck. I don't know where the word *sana* comes from; it is neither butter nor margarine. Occasionally there is a spoonful of jam or sugar. Several times my mother cooks some green tomatoes with a little sugar on the stove in the big room—I love that! But my favorite delicacy is a rind of cheese put on the hot stove until it swells up to twice its size. To bite into that is absolute heaven! Quite a difference from the food we had in prewar days!

Somehow I consider all this normal, as though the prewar time has in some manner slipped my memory. I feel hungry, although not very and not all the time, but I don't ask for food, knowing that there is none. After some weeks I no longer feel hungry. In fact, I eat so little and it becomes so difficult to get me to eat at all that my mother takes me to one of the inmate doctors, who gives me some sort of appetite inducer tasting of cherries. An appetite inducer in a concentration camp with starvation rations! Is there anything more ironic? But it doesn't help. I think I have just pushed the hunger out of my mind and thereby out of my body. Life is easier if I don't also have to deal with hunger.

Games

There is no school during my time in Westerbork, so there is nothing to do. We children just "hang out," to use a modern term, or we occasionally go to the "playground." This is an empty corner of Westerbork where some swings and some teeter-totters have been built, and there is a small sandbox. The sand is polluted and dirty. I sit on the edge of the box one day and watch a boy of about eight or nine relieve himself in the sand, but without removing his pants. Later I see small children play in the sand.

On the whole, however, I do not play very much at all in Westerbork; I don't seem to remember how to play. The other bigger children and I clean the spaces around our beds, sit and talk, or just sit. Once in a while an actor-inmate by the name of Kurt Gerron comes to play with us. He was a very well-known film actor and director in prewar Germany, who appeared in *The Blue Angel* with Marlene Dietrich, among other films. Like my family, he had left Germany and emigrated to Holland, where he, like us, was picked up and deported to Westerbork. Like us, he would be further deported to Theresienstadt. Eventually he would be sent to Auschwitz, where the Nazis would murder him.

What does he play with us? He teaches us songs, he sings them for us and with us, he teaches us dances, and he tells us stories. I remember being with a group of children and him in the middle space between the men's and women's sides of the barracks and dancing in a circle to music. He has no instrument; the music is just us singing. He is very good with us, and very patient. He is not very tall, but he is enormously fat and always wears a pair of khaki-colored shorts.

My father plays a game with me after work as well. He asks me to describe my room for him, just the way it was at home. I have to describe everything very exactly: the furniture, the color, the shape, and where everything stood in the room. I even draw a plan of my room for him. Sometimes he also asks me about the other rooms in the house. In this way he not only keeps my memory sharp, but also reminds me that there had indeed been another time before the war. We talk about school, too—prewar school—and what I learned there. I tell him the plots of books I have read. I tell him about the games Kurt Gerron plays with us. He laughs; Kurt Gerron is a friend of his, and he knows well how funny Gerron can be.

Tensions and Lessons

I do have one friend in Westerbork—not really a good or intimate friend, but a boy I talk with occasionally. His name is Werner, like my cousin's. Our beds are opposite each other, and we talk together when either one of us is ill, or both of us are, which happens often. Most of the talk is fantasy talk, pretending we are somewhere else or that the circumstances are different or our living quarters quieter. There are many quarrels between people in the barracks, between orthodox and non-orthodox Jews, between upper-, middle-, and lower-class people, or between people who want to use the little stove at the same time or who, because of the overcrowding, are forced to hear each other's conversations. My mother does not get on well with our next-bed neighbors: they accuse her of stealing their knife; she accuses them of being rude and loud.

Werner and I see her threatening the bed neighbors with a sort of cheese board made of wood. So Werner and I pretend that none of this exists and that all is normal—which indeed it is, for the place and circumstances we are in, in which all things normal become abnormal and the abnormal is an everyday occurrence. Eventually Werner and his family are deported, and my doll Peter is once again my only friend.

From now on I go with my mother when she takes care of the younger children. I am dressed as she is, in a dark blue training suit, a scarf covering my head, and *klompen* on my feet. The *klompen* are made entirely of wood; they don't give anywhere, and we have to learn to walk in them. In the beginning they are hard on the feet, but after we are used to them we find them very comfortable—at least I do. The top part, however, causes my mother to have a knobby growth of bone on her feet for the rest of her life.

I had always gotten along very well with children younger than I; now I help keep them occupied in some way, clean them after they have soiled themselves, and generally look after them. That, in turn, keeps me occupied and prevents my thinking too much about our situation. Since there is no official school in Westerbork, I am not getting any kind of formal education. I get a different type of education, though. Food is often brought into the camp on trucks from outside. One day I manage to "organize" a cabbage from one of the trucks and bring it triumphantly to the barracks, pleased to add a vegetable to our table, only to be told by my father: My *daughter doesn't steal! Go and take it back immediately!*

Later during the camp years he changed his mind about stealing food, but at this time apparently he was not hungry enough.

Illness and Death

I am ill a good deal in Westerbork, partly with normal children's diseases like measles, partly with things like eczema. What with flea-bites and dirt, any scratch infects very easily, and for months I have my legs in bandages. Of course, we have no regular gauze bandages; the Westerbork variety is made of paper. It looks like toilet paper, only narrower and without the perforations. In order to hold my bandages in place, I may not take off my stockings, else the bandages will come undone as well. The stockings are a pair of purple knee-high socks which I would wear throughout the two years of camp and which I would eventually bring back with me when the war was over. Soon they are no longer purely purple; they are being mended with wool of all colors, including some taken from my doll Peter's green three-piece suit. It is carefully unraveled and used for mending various things, as are all other woolen items we have that are not immediately useful for keeping us clothed.

Other than the sleeping arrangements, which are so different from those I was used to at home, living conditions as a whole are not only different but downright bad. The washroom is but one example. As I mentioned before, it has just the one toilet, therefore we always have to wait in line. In the daytime we can use the outhouse as well, horrible though it is, but at night we may not go out. Therefore, if we need to use the toilet at night, we have to stand in line. The night when I begin to be ill with measles I wake up because I have to use the bathroom, as I am nauseated. As usual there is a long line, but this time I really cannot wait. I bend over the sink and all of a sudden feel a cool hand on my forehead, holding it in the way my mother always holds it when I am sick to my stomach. I look up, but instead of my mother's face I see a stranger's. The woman who holds my head looks as astonished as I must look; just as I think her to be my mother, she thinks me to be her daughter in distress. When she realizes that I am not, she turns away and leaves me to deal with the situation myself. Eventually I am able to go back to bed, but I have to get up twice more during that night.

In the morning, when my mother finds out what happened, she asks, *Why did you not wake me, as I told you to do?*

I did not want to disturb you, Mami. I can go by myself. I'm ten years old.

The outhouse is worse than the toilets in the barracks. It consists of a wooden shack with one side for the men and the other for the women. Inside there is just a sort of shelf with holes in it but without partitions to give privacy. One climbs up on the shelf and squats as best one can, being very careful not to fall in. That this shelf is none too clean, that the smell is none too pleasant—that goes without saying.

As we are allowed to write and receive mail in the camp, I receive several letters from Carla, which I keep very carefully until the day when we have no more toilet paper. Now my precious letters have to be used for that purpose. It is a bad day; I feel that the separation from my old life is now final. It makes me very sad; the friendship between Carla and me has been very important to me, and now I feel as though not only has the friendship terminated, but as though Carla never existed, is a figment of my imagination, just like the stories I tell myself.

Westerbork is supposed to be just a transit camp. Every Tuesday a transport leaves to what we call "the East," or "Poland." Every

Monday evening a list is published with the names of those who are to be deported. In July of 1943, Omi's name appears on the list. Although my father tells her that he will be able to get her off, she does not believe him and takes poison. She dies on July 7, 1943, not quite a month after our arrival in Westerbork.

A Walk and a Drawing

On rare occasions some adult, a teacher perhaps, takes us children on a walk outside the camp. I do not know why the Nazis allow this, but they do. We have to pass through the barbed-wire gate; when we leave, the soldier standing guard counts us, and on our return he counts us again. Naturally the number of children returning has to be the same as the number leaving. Mostly it isn't, and the guard counts us again and again and again until the numbers come out right. Since Westerbork is in the middle of nowhere, and any one of us children would have to flee alone from these walks, running away does not occur to us as a reality. We would be on our own, without parents or siblings; and we know very well that the family members we left behind would be punished. Yet the eternal counting is nerve wracking; I never know nor can I imagine what "they" will do if the number does not eventually come out right.

Will they kill us here and now? Are they going to put us in the S-barracks? How long do we have to stand here? Why can't he count right? Maybe they'll deport us. But where to? To the East, I suppose. I wonder what that's like.

The walks take us onto the heath, of which Drenthe has a lot, and we walk along wooded paths with flowers, blue lupines. We are a group of raggedy-looking children with *klompen* on bare feet, our clothes have holes, as do our feet where the wood of the *klompen* has rubbed them raw. Many of the children are ill with diarrhea and have lost all control of their bowels. The backs of their legs are stained brown, their wet clothes have stiffened and chafe against their bodies, causing more holes and infections. Sometimes during these walks we sit down to rest in a field of blue lupines. Because of the association of lupines with these walks, I dislike those flowers even today, though I love flowers in general.

One of the women in our barracks is an artist. It seems to me that she is tall and has dark hair and rather a long face. She smiles at me. For some reason she wants to draw me and asks my parents for permission to do so. So there I sit at one of the wooden tables, trying to keep a smile on my face because I think that's what she wants. Eventually she tells me not to smile, just to look the way I always look. For the portrait I wear the cardigan I always wear in Westerbork: dark blue with red and yellow rectangles knitted into it all over. It has gold-colored buttons down the front and two pockets, one on either side. I don't know where it came from, whether it has always been mine or whether I "inherited" it from someone else; but I do know that I wore it day in, day out, and that it came back with me, after our liberation, to Amsterdam, where I wore it for several more years. It must have grown with me, for I do not remember it ever being too small.

The drawing is eventually finished, charcoal or dark pencil on grayish paper. What happened to it? I don't know; the artist wanted to keep it, and I do not know her fate.

Showers and Noise

From time to time, at irregular intervals, we are told that it is time to take a shower. There are two types of showers in Westerbork. One is a big room with shower heads coming out of the ceiling. Twenty or more women can and do shower at once in that room. Those who have a child, like my mother, have to share their shower with the child. The water comes on and all the women move under the stream, wet the soap, and start washing. The water then stops and does not come back on until it is rinsing time. I am horrified by all the nude women, not because they are nude, but because of the way they look—the same way we also look, with sagging skin, sagging breasts, and too many wrinkles. Later, in private, I tell my mother, *Mami, I don't ever want to look that way, my skin so loose and my breasts hanging down.*

I don't realize yet that I have no say over that. I also do not realize, cannot know, that I haven't really seen the worst yet. That is still to come, later in Theresienstadt. Their bodies are bloated, too, and the voices with which they call out to each other while showering are shrill to my child's ears. I like the shower and the clean feeling after, but I hate to go into that big room.

The other type of shower is "private," that is, it is a small cubicle with just one shower head and just enough room for one person. The guard turns the water on in all the cubicles simultaneously. My mother and I have to share the shower, of course, just as in the big room. Again the water comes on and then is turned off until the guard thinks we ought to be ready to rinse, then she turns it on again. Her voice floats in: *"Nog drie minuten, dames!"* "Three more minutes, ladies!" Then the water is turned off, whether we are rinsed and ready or not. If we have to wash our hair, the time barely suffices. Then the walk back to the barracks in our robes or whatever we wear and our *klompen*. In winter there is quite a difference in temperature; the showers have warm water, but the outside air is cold (the winter of 1943-1944 was a very cold winter in Holland). If we have wet hair, we are practically frozen by the time we get back to the barracks.

For haircuts, or if we have lice and have to get all our hair shaved off, we go to a red tent which is erected at irregular intervals somewhere in the camp. It's easy to tell who had lice and now has a shaven head; the women and children then wear a scarf knotted in a very particular way and covering the whole head. The men, of course, do not wear anything on their heads; they are just bald.

Other than these very specific things, what I most remember about Westerbork is noise. Noise and crowds. Crowds everywhere. Crowds of people in the barracks, crowds of people outside, crowds of people walking along the railroad tracks running through the center of the camp, crowds of people in long lines waiting to get some hot water from a faucet located near a tall red-brick chimney (the kitchen?), crowds of people waiting in long lines to use the toilet or the outhouse. Crowds everywhere. So many people, so many voices, so many quarrels, so much noise. The noise never stops. It is never silent in the barracks. Even at night when I wake up, people are talking, crying, groaning, snoring. There simply is no privacy, and for me, an only child who had my own room at home and who comes from a very private family, this is one of the worst things in Westerbork. We all had lots of space at home; here we have none.

We Leave Westerbork

I was about to discover, however, that Westerbork was not, by any means, the worst place to be, for all that it was so bad. I was about to find out—we were all about to find out—that whatever privations Westerbork held for us were as nothing compared to where we were going—and that was not the worst place, either.

In the early part of January 1944, my father received an order to go and see the commandant of Westerbork. It caused great anxiety, for those orders could bring nothing but bad news. My father lay in his bunk with a high fever, and so could not follow this order. He sent a message to that effect, but remained trembling because no one knew how that kind of message would be received. Surprisingly, it was accepted, and my father remained in his bunk for several more days. Eventually, when he got better, he went to see the commandant. Meanwhile, on January 11, 1944, a transport had left Westerbork bound for Bergen-Belsen. Since my father had not yet kept his appointment, we were not on that transport. Instead we were deported on the next transport, which left on January 18, 1944. It was bound for Theresienstadt, in Czechoslovakia.

A total of 102,000 persons, the great majority of them Jews but also about 200 Gypsies and an unknown number of resistance fighters, perished, either in Westerbork itself or as a result of being deported to other camps like Auschwitz, Sobibor, and others.

Transport leaving Westerbork.
This was not our transport to Theresienstadt,
but the photo shows how transports typically left.

Theresienstadt

JANUARY 20, 1944–JUNE 1945

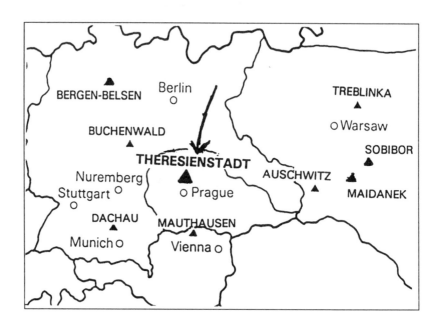

ABOVE: *Partial map of Europe with some of the concentration camps.*
Theresienstadt is shown by an arrow.

BELOW: *The rampart walls surrounding Theresienstadt. Although there is*
grass on top (and outside), they looked very threatening to me
from inside the concentration camp. (Photo taken by my cousin.)

Theresienstadt:
History and Description

Theresienstadt was founded in 1780 by the Austrian emperor Joseph II and named after his mother, Maria Theresa. In Czech it is known as Terezín. It was a small fortified town with a big fortress on one side and a little fortress on the other side of the river Ohre. Since it was never besieged, the fortress was abolished in 1882, but Theresienstadt remained a small military town with a garrison of about 3,500 soldiers and a civilian population of about 3,700 as of 1940. The fortress was built in the shape of a twelve-pointed star, the size of which was approximately 1,400 by 1,020 yards. The size of the town within the rampart walls was approximately 800 yards in length by approximately 600 yards in width. The streets were straight and intersected at right angles; there were seven streets in the long direction and nine cross streets. They were paved badly or not at all, with the result that on dry days dust whirled about, and when it rained the streets became rivers of mud. None of this changed in 1941 when the town became a "ghetto"—the official name the Nazis gave it.

There were 219 buildings in the garrison town, mostly barracks for the soldiers, but also some private houses for the civilians. The barracks were massive buildings of red or yellow stone approximately twenty-five to thirty-eight feet high. They were hardly suitable for living quarters, as they were very dark, damp, and cold inside and had neither heat nor running water. Water had to be hauled from a pump in the middle of the square courtyard around which the barracks were built. Most of them dated from the eighteenth century. Most of the private houses were over one hundred years old; they had two floors, were very narrow and uncomfortable, and lacked all modern sanitation. None of this changed, either, when Theresienstadt became a "ghetto." With the existing sanitary facilities there were, in 1942, 988 toilet facilities for 53,000 prisoners, or one toilet for every fifty-four people. Most of these were not flush toilets.

In 1941 the garrison was withdrawn so that Theresienstadt could be used by the Nazis for the detention of Jews. Modern ghettos, as set up by the Nazis, were in fact places of detention where those people were sent who were defined as Jews by the racial laws of Nazi Germany. They had been forcibly deported from their homes and in many cases from their countries. There were very few differences between that type of ghetto and "Ghetto Theresienstadt." No one was ever released from a ghetto; the inhabitants were not permitted to have any contact with people outside the walls, on threat of severe penalties, and no one could act out of choice. All of this was equally true of Theresienstadt. Although the Nazis called the town "Ghetto Theresienstadt," it was in actual fact a concentration camp. According to the 1940 figures, there were then about 7,200 people living in the town; the Nazis crowded, at a minimum, over 11,000 people into the same quarters. Mostly, however, that was an ideal. Usually there were over 60,000 prisoners in Theresienstadt at the same time, in this town which had been built for 7,000. A total of 15,000 children under fifteen years old went through Theresienstadt; of these a little over 100 survived.[3]

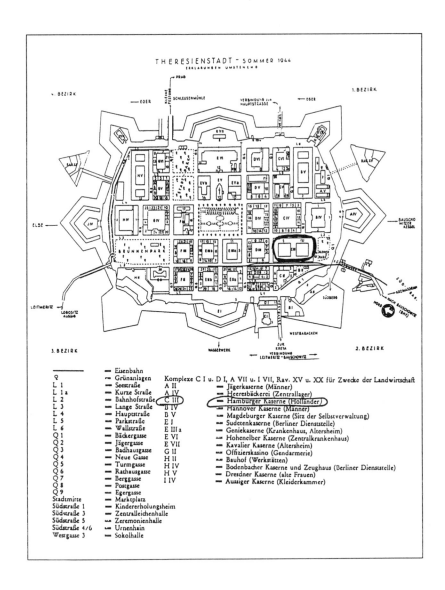

Map of Theresienstadt as found in Adler's two books.
The Hamburger Kaserne (Hamburg Barracks), where we were quartered
after our arrival, is circled.

Entrance to the Small Fortress, through which we entered Theresienstadt.
As on entrances to other concentration camps,
here also the inscription reads:
"Work makes one free."

Transport and Arrival

We were deported from Westerbork on January 18, 1944. We arrived in Theresienstadt, Czechoslovakia, on January 20 after a nightmare trip of two days. Most of that trip has escaped my memory; I have images in my mind of cattle cars and long stretches of time in darkness, but not much else. Did we arrive in the daytime? At night? I no longer know. I only know that we did arrive, finally.

As at Westerbork, we had to go through some sort of "registration" and "disinfection," which at Theresienstadt were called *Schleuse*, the sluice. In the process of "disinfection," the greater part of those things we still owned disappeared. In this concentration camp there was a special verb for this: *schleusen*, to sluice (or to be sluiced), indicating the stealing which took place upon people's arrival.

•

I follow my mother around and go wherever she goes. My father has disappeared; we eventually find out that he has been assigned to a different barracks. My mother and I are assigned to the Hamburger Kaserne, or Hamburg Barracks, together with the other inmates from Holland. Here we find ourselves in a room with about fifty or so other women and children; my father is quartered in a similar room in his barracks, but with men and boys over twelve years old. Men and women are kept separated; boys under twelve stay with their mothers. Men's and women's living quarters were

RIJKSINSTITUUT VOOR

OORLOGSDOCUMENTATIE

NETHERLANDS STATE INSTITUTE FOR WAR DOCUMENTATION
INSTITUT NATIONAL NÉERLANDAIS POUR LA DOCUMENTATION DE GUERRE
NIEDERLÄNDISCHES STAATLICHES INSTITUT FÜR KRIEGSDOKUMENTATION

OVERZICHT VAN DE UIT NEDERLAND

GEDEPORTEERDE JODEN

Datum	Aantal gedeporteerden	Kamp
14- 9-1943	305	Theresienstadt
21- 9-1943	979	Auschwitz
19-10-1943	1007	"
15-11-1943	1149	"
16-11-1943	995	"
11- 1-1944	1037	Bergen-Belsen
18- 1-1944	870	Theresienstadt
25- 1-1944	949	Auschwitz
1- 2-1944	908	Bergen-Belsen
8- 2-1944	1015	Auschwitz
15- 2-1944	773	Bergen-Belsen
25- 2-1944	811	Theresienstadt
3- 3-1944	732	Auschwitz
15- 3-1944	210	Bergen-Belsen
23- 3-1944	599	Auschwitz
5- 4-1944	289	Theresienstadt
5- 4-1944	240	Auschwitz
5- 4-1944	101	Bergen-Belsen

Partial list of deportation transports leaving Holland;
the transport by which we were deported to Theresienstadt is circled.

Designation	Date of Arrival	Number of Deportees
14g	2.4.43	72
EZ	28.4.43	2
IV/14h	27.5.43	205
EZ	17.6.43	3
IV/14i	26.6.43	152
IV/14k	16.7.43	17
IV/14l	3.9.43	20
IV/14m	10.9.43	10
EZ	16.9.43	1
IV/14n	12.11.43	91
IV/14o	1.12.43	46
EZ	15.12.43	1
IV/14p	11.1.44	6
EZ	20.1.44	1
IV/15	11.3.44	84
IV/15b	29.4.44	80
IV/14p	18.5.44	1
IV/14p	19.5.44	4
IV/14p	3.6.44	1
IV/14p	22.6.44	4
IV/14p	10.7.44	5
IV/14p	24.7.44	1
IV/15d	17.8.44	16
IV/14p	22.9.44	2
IV/14p	21.11.44	4
IV/14p	23.11.44	1
IV/15d	2.2.45	4
IV/15e	16.2.45	7
IV/16	8.3.45	1073
IV/17	20.3.45	11
IV/16a	15.4.45	77

Designation	Date of Arrival	Number of Deportees
HOLLAND (Amsterdam, The Hague, Naarden, Westerbork)		
XXIV/1	22.2.43	295
EZ	27.5.43	2
XXIV/2	20.1.44	870
XXIV/3	27.1.44	283
XXIV/4	26.2.44	809
XXIV/5	7.4.44	289
XXIV/3	12.7.44	3
XXIV/6	2.8.44	213
EZ	2.8.44	1
XXIV/7	6.9.44	2081
XXIV/8	20.11.44	51
DENMARK (Abo, Frederiksberg, Copenhagen, Odense)		
XXV/1	5.10.43	83
XXV/2	6.10.43	198
XXV/3	14.10.43	175
XXV/4	13.1.44	8
EZ	25.4.44	2
SLOVAKIA (Sered)		
XXVI/1	23.12.44	416
XXVI/2	19.1.45	129
XXVI/3	12.3.45	548
XXVI/4	7.4.45	354

Partial list of transports arriving in Theresienstadt;
the transport by which we arrived is circled.
From the dates on the two partial lists, it can be seen that
it took two days to go from Westerbork to Theresienstadt.

always kept separate, to my knowledge, and most of the children were not kept with their parents but were quartered in what was euphemistically called a *Kinderheim*, or children's home. In several barracks rooms were put aside for that purpose, each room overseen by an adult who might have been a teacher in prewar life, but might equally well have been just any adult.

I am lucky in that I stay with my mother in the big room. This type of room has a wooden floor, and we have bunk beds as we did in Westerbork, with either two or three tiers, placed against the walls all around the room. We have a little less than three feet between tiers, and each bed is a little over two feet wide. That is all the space we are allowed. Once again there are no closets or anything like that, and we have to keep all our possessions, such as they are, in and on the bed. The bunks are made of wood and cannot ever be rid of vermin; bedbugs make their home inside the wood, fleas inhabit the straw-sack mattresses, and lice are ever present. In each room there is a *Zimmeraelteste*, or elder of the room, who rations out necessary items such as soap or sanitary napkins and the occasional bit of toilet paper. We receive a small piece of *"Luftseife,"* "air-soap," every six or seven weeks. It is brown in color and we call it "air-soap" because when water runs on it, it collapses like a balloon when the air is let out of it. Everything has to be washed with this soap, including our food containers, and all washing must be done in the washrooms. These resemble the ones in Westerbork: long sinks with many faucets which give cold water only, if any. There are several toilets in the Hamburger Barracks washroom, but without partitions between them, so we have no privacy for even this function.

We have a curfew here: the lights have to be out at ten o'clock. In the women's quarters, two women have *Zimmerdienst*, room duty, every morning; they have to sweep and clean the room. In the men's quarters this is done by women as well—by the so-called *Putzkolonne*, the cleaning crew. The *Putzkolonne* also has to clean the halls, the offices, and the sick-rooms. A special *Putzkolonne* goes to clean the Nazi headquarters in Theresienstadt. Neither they nor anyone else can ever really get rid of the enormous quantities of dirt and vermin, even though whole buildings are disinfected now and then. When that happens we are warned, ironically, by yellow sheets of paper with a skull and cross-bones on it and the following text: "*Achtung! Vorsicht! Durchgasung mit* GIFTGAS*! Lebensgefahr—Zutritt strengstens verboten!*"[4] "Attention! Caution! Fumigating with POISON GAS! Danger of death—entry strictly forbidden!"

Bunk beds as used in Theresienstadt;
contrary to Westerbork, where they were made of metal,
these are built of wood and provided a wonderful home for bedbugs.
(Photo taken by my cousin.)

Hans and I

Immediately after our arrival in the big room, my mother and I make friends with another woman and her young son, who is two years younger than I. Her husband and elder son, who is one year older than I, are in the men's quarters. The younger boy, whose name is Hans, and I become heart friends very quickly. From the beginning we are inseparable.

Hans has light brown hair and brown eyes that almost always have a question in them. He is smaller than I am, though equally skinny. Hans is everything to me: brother, playmate, confidante; had we been older, we certainly would have been lovers. But we are too young for that, although we do talk about getting married after the war when we grow up.

Hans is a real friend, even though my doll Peter is still always with me. But Hans can do things Peter can never do. With Hans I can have real discussions; I get real answers and can ask real questions. Hans goes where I go, and I go where he goes. We do our chores together, go get food together, occasionally play together, spin fantasies together, talk together a little about "before the war" and sometimes about "after the war," although neither of us really knows when that will be or how it will be.

One of the places where we go regularly is up to the top floor of the barracks. There, in the attic four floors up, there are open arches in the walls, almost like doorways. Perhaps in peacetime they were used to haul things up by means of pulleys. In any event, these arches are not barricaded in any way, and Hans and I often stand in them. We look down on the courtyard or out to where Theresienstadt ends, where the fortress walls signal the boundary between Theresienstadt and the rest of the world, and we pretend we can fly. We know it's only pretend flying, but it's such a lovely dream. We can go wherever we want: we can fly away from here, to any place we want, any place where it is not filthy, crowded, and noisy, and where we can be alone. We can fly away home. It is a wonderful dream.

The attics are also used as living spaces. There are some rooms in the corners, but the rest is open space with just beams connecting the walls. The floor is lower under these beams, and we have to be careful not to fall into the open spaces when we walk on the beams, which we regularly do—it is a game all the children play. In the lower, open spaces live rat families. We make a game of poking at them with a stick to make them move or jump. Surprisingly, they never harm or attack us; I imagine that even the rats do not have enough to eat here and are, as we are, weak from hunger. But it is one of our favorite games, and we are never bored with it.

Hans and I dream a lot together, mostly about where to "organize" more food or about what we'll do after the war. Armed with some sort of container—a light blue pillow case for me—we go to the railroad station to search for food. Actually, it isn't a station so much as just a rail spur going into Theresienstadt, though I didn't learn that until after the war. To us it is "the" station; both people and goods arrive there. Sometimes we are lucky: we find a potato or a cabbage. It may be putrid, but it can still be eaten. Naturally, we make a game of it, as we do with many other things. The game is to see who can find more. Should we get caught, we and our families would be severely punished by the Nazis. It would mean transport to the East, or to the "Small Fortress," where people are tortured. It might even mean being shot. But our hunger drives us on, and we keep going.

In the course of going anywhere in Theresienstadt, one has to salute when the Nazis go by. Hans and I make a game out of that, too. Who can salute better, stand straighter, and keep a straighter face?

For some reason my family is moved to a small "private" room, still in the Hamburg Barracks, and perhaps once an officer's quarters. We share it with Hans and his mother. The three adults all have their own beds; Hans and I have a two-tiered bunk bed. One of our favorite early-morning games is to hunt for fleas and bedbugs. The game consists first of deciding what to catch first, fleas or bedbugs. That decided, we set a certain amount of time, catch and kill as fast as we can, put them aside, and when the time is up, count them. Whoever has more wins the game. It's not a difficult game; it doesn't even take any skill. Both fleas and bedbugs are plentiful, and all we need is speed to outcatch the other. It's not even a fun game, but it makes a game out of a necessity, so we play determinedly every morning.

Did we get the fleas from our rat playmates? Perhaps; but we would get them anyway. In Theresienstadt with its overcrowded quarters, its overcrowded streets, that human antheap whose inhabitants keep moving to keep living, everyone is at all times so close together that everyone catches every vermin and every disease caught by even one inmate.

Though Hans and I talk a lot about "After the war...," we don't really know if or when that will be. We talk about going back to Holland. After the war we'll go back to school, but neither of us *really* remembers just what that's like. After the war we'll have our own rooms again, although we don't *really* remember what that feels like, either. After the war we'll play in the street again. After the war we'll get married; we know we want to spend our lives together. We also know that we have to grow up first, but that doesn't seem to be a problem: already we're well on our way. But sometimes we just sit and don't talk at all; we're just together.

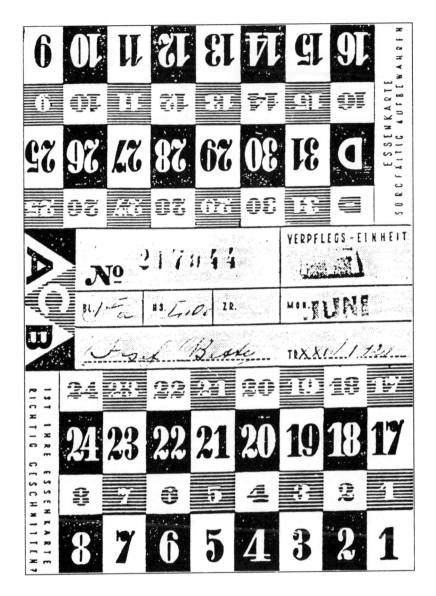

Ration card for meals, as used in Theresienstadt.
The card had to be handed over at every meal distribution,
and the appropriate number would be cut off.

Food

Hans and I also think about food. My mother is part of the *Putzkolonne* who has to clean the Nazi headquarters. Every once in a while she brings back some chestnuts (horse chestnuts) she has found during her cleaning and smuggled out of the building. Hans and I use a knife to shape them into baskets and other things. Then, in our imagination, we fill the baskets with food. We think about food a lot; it's a major preoccupation since we never have enough. We don't have fantasies about having *what* we want—we don't think about cake or chocolate. We just think about having *all* we want and feeling sated. But, like flying, that never happens either.

One of our chores is to go and fetch food for our families. For this purpose we carry an *etensdrager*, or food carrier in Dutch, a sort of wooden tray with a barrier on all four sides so that the pots cannot slide off and a wooden handle by which to carry it. We take our food coupons with us and stand in line with many others at the Magdeburger Kaserne, the Magdeburg Barracks, to wait for the food to be given out. In the process we have to defend our place in line because we are "only children," and therefore any adult can shove us out of line and take our place. We learn very quickly to defend ourselves; the wooden *etensdrager* is a wonderful weapon. When our turn comes, we give our fullest attention to what the server ladles into our pots. Actually, our attention is held less by *what* he is ladling out than by *how much* he is ladling out. We are three people; Hans and his mother are two; we always have to make sure to get our full share of three and two ladles full, respectively.

We make a game out of this chore, too. Sometimes the guard forgets to ask for our coupons, so naturally we do not offer them voluntarily. It means that we can then go through another line with another guard and get another portion. The game is to see who of the two of us is luckier or better at it.

What is it we get? It may be "potato soup" (though I cannot remember ever seeing a potato in it; at most a piece of potato peel) or barley soup. Sometimes it is a sort of cereal, greenish-yellow in color; I don't even know what it is made of, but I like it. On very rare occasions we receive a *Buchtel*, a square bakery item which holds the middle between a large biscuit and a pastry. There is "coffee" for adults, which is black and watery; what it is in reality I don't know. There are turnips as well; they are cooked, but stone hard, and are a dull orange in color. We get them often, but they are mostly either unripe or rotten.

Other Games

Hans and I play a number of other games as well, games we invent ourselves. For example, there is a Dutch song about a dog who is very cute when he is small, but as he gets bigger and bigger his bark gets louder and louder and he is no longer quite so cute. Together we act out the happenings in the song; I can't sing, so Hans sings the song while I play the dog, providing barks from very high yelps to deep, growly barks, as with every stanza I grow a little.

We play with my doll as well, although I do not remember any specific games. Mostly we try to trade some of Peter's non-woolen clothes for other, woolen ones. That wool can be used for other things. We unravel the clothes and I use the wool to mend my father's stockings and my own. I still have the same purple knee-high stockings I had in Westerbork, but now they are patched in a rainbow of green, yellow, red, and blue. Any color will do; it's terribly important for us children to have more color patches in our socks than any other child—another typical camp game.

One game that I play only once, perhaps after Hans' deportation, has to do with a stamp. It's always very important to possess something which other children do not have, and a lot of trading goes on. One day I see that one of the children has a postage stamp. Where he got it I don't know, but I desperately want it because it is bright and has many colors. I enter into negotiations to exchange some doll clothes for the stamp. Once I have the stamp in my hand, though, I run away as fast as I can without giving up the doll clothes. The group of children runs after me and eventually catches me. By then I have hidden the stamp in the inner pocket of my coat, and the children never find it. (The coat is a boys' coat which I inherited from my cousin.) I remain triumphant.

Hans and I have another game—really a kind of non-game. It is, in effect, a non-everything; it consists of all those things we know but do *not* talk about. We do not talk about transports; we do not mention people who have disappeared; we do not discuss what it might be like in the East. We don't know anybody who has ever come back to Theresienstadt from "Poland," therefore we know that wherever and whatever it is, it is a dangerous place. We have heard rumors about gas chambers, and although we cannot imagine what they look like, we know that they kill. We also know that death is permanent; in our roamings through Theresienstadt we see the dead stacked on open carts, and we know they are taken to the crematorium.

We also know about the "Small Fortress" where people are sent as punishment and where they are beaten and tortured. Most of them do not come back to the camp proper, either.

All these things we know in our minds and our souls, but they remain part of our silent knowledge. We have no need to talk about them; they are part of our everyday life, and as such they are taken for granted. So this game is one we don't play. The silence is the game. We are both very good at it.

My Four Companions

From the beginning of my time in Theresienstadt I have four companions in addition to Hans. Later, when Hans is gone, they will become even more important, but they are with me from the day I arrive. Two of them are not really *friends*, but they are close acquaintances until they, too, disappear. The other two become close friends. They are with me every day and every night; they never leave me, so I am never alone.

Hunger is the first one to appear. He is small in the beginning, though larger than he was in Westerbork. Now Hunger grows by leaps and bounds; he is in his element here. He teases me, sometimes cruelly, by talking to me about food, food past and present. He tortures me mentally by keeping images of food in front of my eyes. He also tortures me physically: he pinches me, stabs me, gives me all sorts of pain. He keeps me tired all the time. Of course, he tortures everyone here, but I don't know how the adults feel. They don't tell me; in fact, they don't talk about this unwelcome fellow at all. Does he pinch them, too? Does he stab them? Or does he torture them in a different way? Neither Mami nor Papi talk about it or even mention him. So I don't mention my companion to them either; I think they have other worries, and I don't need to talk about him. In any event, it wouldn't help; Hunger stays with all of us, whether we like him or not. So I try to disregard Hunger, but do not always succeed; it takes more work here to shut him out than it took in Westerbork.

Eventually, after a longish time, my second companion ousts Hunger, but becomes herself tormentor and torment at the same time. Her name is Fear. She is stronger than Hunger in her control over both my mind and my body. Of course, I have now a weaker body; she does not have to work as hard as Hunger. I do not like her any better than I like Hunger, so I don't mention her either. Besides, I think that maybe she visits Mami and Papi, too—although again I don't really know, for they say nothing. Still, for all my dislike of her, I am grateful that she has chased Hunger away. In spite of Fear's control over me, I look for food or for items barterable for food, for fuel, or for anything that might prove useful in this existence. She keeps my body limber so that I can flee at the smallest sign of danger, but she occupies my mind fully. At least she doesn't torture my body, so I have gained in the exchange. Still, I cannot seem to think of anyone but her. She makes me look over my shoulder all the time to see whether anyone sees what I am doing or where I am going. This is not to my liking, so I ask my third companion to help me conquer Fear.

Cold and Fear struggle for a long time. Sometimes one of them gets the upper hand, sometimes, the other. Cold wins after several long battles, and I am happy with his victory. He now takes me in hand; in fact, he takes me over. He caresses me from top to bottom so that I no longer feel the previous abuse from Hunger and Fear. This I like; it makes me feel more peaceful, less struggling, and therefore stronger, less tired. He not only strokes my body; he strokes my mind, and a miracle happens: I am freed from Hunger and Fear. Cold's fingers numb me; I do not have many clothes, but I do not feel uncomfortable even though it is winter and there is snow on the ground. I do not eat much, since there isn't much, but I do not feel the lack. I still go searching for food and other useful items, but though I know that the consequences of being caught may be beatings or a bullet, Cold leaves my mind free of Fear so that I can pay more attention to what I am doing. I like Cold very much; he is a true friend.

My fourth companion is the best, because she is the most caring. She walks on my right side, she holds me by the hand or keeps her hand on my shoulder or on my head. She comforts me by numbing the last bit of me which Cold has not been able to reach. She plays with me, stays with me when I go to bed at night, rocks me and sings me to sleep. She is with me when I awaken in the morning, smiles at me and holds out her hand to help me up. She teaches me to welcome her, not ever to be afraid of her, no matter in what form she presents herself. I see her in many forms: starvation, disease, beatings, hangings. I see so much of these that I don't really pay attention to them. They are, after all, everyday sights, as natural to Theresienstadt as the Nazis passing by. I see the result of her touch: those who have gone away with her are taken away on open carts drawn through town by camp inmates. I do not want to go with her; I do not go looking for her, but she comes to me without my asking. I do welcome her care though; no one else has much time to care for me. Her name is Death, and she is my most loyal friend.

Daily Activities

Most of the time I am alone. Technically speaking, this is not quite true, for after all, my parents are also in Theresienstadt, and I stay with them. Yet because they are working, it is up to me to clean the space around our beds (my mother's and mine), to make the beds, and to do those household tasks which normally my mother would do. I take her place in sweeping the floor or scrubbing it with Lysol in water and a big broom. As best I can, I fix whatever tears or holes we have in our clothes, and I mend our socks. At about noon and in the evening I go to fetch our food from the Magdeburg Barracks.

·

In the beginning, my mother was part of the *Putzkolonne*. Later she was reassigned to work in the *Glimmer* industry, the mica industry. Mica is one of a group of minerals which separate easily into thin and tough layers. The layers are transparent, and the Nazis used this material for their war industry. The women in the mica industry had to separate the mica layers. There were three shifts of eight hours, so the work continued twenty-four hours a day.

My father started out by being a street cleaner, armed with a sort of cart, a shovel, and a broom made of twigs. Later he too was reassigned and became Theresienstadt's pharmacist. There were practically no medications in the camp, but the Nazis had set a space aside for those medications that came from inmates' luggage, and

PERSONENBESCHREIBUNG

Statur	gross
Haare	braun
Augen	grün
Bart	keinen
Gesicht	länglich
Zähne	schadhaft
Nase	normal
Mund	normal
Bes. Kennzeichen	
	keine

GHETTO THERESIENSTADT
Der Ältestenrat
G. Z. 1534-7760/44

II. M. XIV-2
wohnt Langestr. 5/M 7

Ausweis.

Name u. Vorname: Silten Ilse S.

geboren am: 23.2.09 in Berlin   Staatsang.: Staatenlos

Heim. Gemeinde: --   Stand: Verheiratet

letzte Wohnadresse: Westerbork

wird in Theresienstadt unter Tr. Nr. 630/XXIV-2 im Stande geführt.

Dieser Ausweis wurde auf Grund der Transportliste, der Familien-kartei und der eidesstattlichen Erklärung des Ausweisinhabers ausgestellt.

Theresienstadt, am 10.3.1944.

Der Ältestenrat

My mother's Theresienstadt identification card, with a photo of her in 1944 at age thirty-five. The transport number (bottom half, fourth line from bottom) was used as an I.D. number.

PERSONENBESCHREIBUNG:

Statur	gross
Haare	braun
Augen	grün
Bart	keinen
Gesicht	länglich
Zähne	ausgebessert
Nase	gebogen
Mund	normal
Bes. Kennzeichen	
	keine

Eigenhändige Unterschrift des Ausweisinhabers.

GHETTO THERESIENSTADT
Der Ältestenrat
G. Z. 15o7-7746/44

Tr. Nr. 629/XXIV-2

wohnt Langestr. 5/241

Ausweis.

Name u. Vorname: Silten Fritz I.

geboren am: 16.2.o4 *in* Berlin   *Staatsang.:* Staatenlos

Heim. Gemeinde: --   *Stand:* Verheiratet

letzte Wohnadresse: Westerbork

wird in Theresienstadt unter Tr. Nr. 629/XXIV-2 *im Stande geführt.*

Dieser Ausweis wurde auf Grund der Transportliste, der Familien-
kartei und der eidesstattlichen Erklärung des Ausweisinhabers ausgestellt.

Theresienstadt, am 1o.3.1944.   *Der Ältestenrat*

My father's Theresienstadt identification card, with a photo of him in 1944
at age forty. The transport number (bottom half, fourth line from bottom)
was used as an I.D. number.

this space was called the pharmacy. Here my father worked with an assistant whose name I have unfortunately forgotten but who was a goldsmith in prewar life.

Because of these occupations, my parents were gone most of the day.

•

On one of the days when we receive a *Buchtel*, a room neighbor asks me to go and pick hers up for her daughter.

Would you go and pick up Ellen's Buchtel for her? I cannot go; I'm not feeling well.

All right, I'll go for you, Mrs. Dornfeld. Do you want me to go right now?

Yes, can you?

Yes.

And off I go, Mrs. Dornfeld's coupons clutched in my hand. Unfortunately, I'm very hungry, as always, and I have to stand in line a long time. One the way back to the barracks, I try very hard not to bite into the Buchtel. I try to think of other things. But before I know it, I have bitten off one of the corners. It doesn't help very much, and pretty soon a second corner has disappeared. When I return to the barracks, Mrs. Dornfeld is furious with me.

You stupid girl, what have you done? That wasn't your Buchtel to eat; you were sent to get it for my daughter. You naughty child, what shall I tell her now? Really, you are very bad!

I make things worse by saying the first thing that comes into my head:

Oh, Mrs. Dornfeld, they gave it to me this way. I didn't do anything to it. I didn't bite into it. I wouldn't do that.

•

It never did occur to me that Mrs. Dornfeld would see my tooth marks in the *Buchtel*, of course. Lying came easily to me in those days; I had learned my school lessons very well.

My mother and I were quartered in an attic when that happened;

we had moved several times, for various reasons. The attic was in the Dresdner Kaserne. We had no beds there; our straw-sack mattresses lay directly on the wooden floor all in a row. While we were in that attic, something else happened, something that was a typical child-turned-adult mistake. My mother had left some water in one of our drinking cups with a small piece of soap in it, which she hoped would dissolve while she was at work so that on her return to the barracks she could use the soapy water to wash her hair. Unfortunately, she didn't tell me anything about it, and in my daily tidying up I found the cup and threw away half the water before I saw the sliver of soap and realized that it had a use. When my mother came back after work I told her what I had done. I could see that she was disappointed, but she didn't say anything about it. Still, I can see her disappointed face even today.

For a while we were quartered in another attic, in our original Hamburg Barracks. We stayed there quite a long time. Again we had no beds, and the room in which we slept had a tiled floor, unlike the attic in the Dresden Barracks, perhaps because these rooms were originally used for storage. Here, too, our straw sacks were all in a row on the floor. This room had a tiny stove in it; we were able to burn something in that—wood most likely—so that we had a very small space where we could warm our hands.

•

One day my mother asks me to wash a handkerchief for her. I do this, then try to dry it in front of this tiny heater. Naturally I am not the only one who wants to be close to it; there are several women trying to get some warmth as well. I spread out my handkerchief and stand somewhat to the side. One of the older women comes to sit down in front of the heater; she really spreads herself out, but she cannot get all the warmth she wants.

You, child, get out of my way! I want to sit here!

But Mami told me to wash and dry her handkerchief for her. I can't do that all the way on the side.

Get out of my way, I say! I want the heat!

But...

No buts! Just get out of the way!

The other women don't intervene; either they're not interested or they don't want to get involved in a quarrel between an older woman and a child; after all, I *am* only a child! But at that moment, my rage overwhelms me. I hardly know what I am doing when I pick up a low stool and threaten the older woman with it. I hold it high above my head and advance toward her.

My mami told me to dry her handkerchief and I am not going out of your way!

The older woman sees that I am serious and likely to throw the stool at her any minute. As close as I am standing to her, I cannot miss. She moves away, and I finish drying my mother's handkerchief. When my mother comes back, I present her with it, very proudly. I don't say anything about the quarrel, however, and I have never known whether she found out, whether the older woman or any of the others ever told her about it.

My Eleventh Birthday

Today is my birthday. I wake up with a feeling that something important is happening, but I'm not sure what. Mami comes and says *Happy birthday!* and so does Papi. I am polite and say *Thank you*, even though I'm not at all sure what I am thanking them for. It is my birthday. What is a birthday? It's the day on which I was born eleven years ago, so long ago that those years recede in the distance, like a long, long road, so long that I cannot see the end—or is it the beginning—which is lost in the mist? Why is it important that I was born on this day? What is supposed to happen today? Is today different from all other days?

I get up slowly, go down to the washroom (we are still in the attic) and wash with the usual icy water. I put on the only clothes I have: a pair of dark blue shorts and a blouse, and I put my bare feet in my wooden shoes brought from Westerbork. I don't put on my stockings; they need to be mended, even though every time I put a needle in them I create a new hole. Therefore I only wear them on special occasions, and also because they have become a bit small by now. Is today a special occasion? I don't know, but I don't think so. So I go without stockings.

I drink some of the "soup" we get in the morning and set about cleaning our space, as I do every morning. I make my bed and Mami's bed. Then I pour Lysol in a pail of water, sprinkle some of the water on the wooden floor, then sweep the floor as best I can.

Naturally, the neighbor woman complains that I raise too much dust. I don't listen to her; she always complains. When I have finished I go in search of Hans, and together we go to see if we can "organize" some food somewhere. Today we are not lucky; we find nothing. We search for coal or wood for heating; we find nothing. At the appointed time we go to stand in the food line at the Magdeburg Barracks. The man asks us for our coupons, so today we cannot go through the line twice. We take our food carriers back to the barracks and eat our portions.

Then, after a while, I find myself alone; I don't know where Hans has gone. I am sitting on the bed when Hans' mother comes to me and says *Happy birthday!* and gives me a present. At first I don't understand that it is a present, but then she says, *This is for you, for your birthday!* I look at her, amazed; I can hardly believe that she would give me this gift. Surely this is too good to be true; she will snatch it away as soon as I stretch out my hand. But she nods to me again and again, and finally I stretch out my hand, still fearful that this is a dream. But it isn't, and she hands me my present.

Thank you, I say softly, and I look at what I hold now. It is half a piece of our usual black "bread," and she has scraped some margarine on it and put some grains of sugar on it as well. I would like to share it with Hans, but I am too hungry. I cannot even make it last very long; it is gone in a few bites. I know that she has saved the bread, the margarine, and the sugar very carefully over several days; I know that she has had less to eat so that she could give me this present. Now, after I finish it, I hug her tightly. Maybe birthdays *are* special days, after all. I try to remember birthdays from previous years, but it's all gone. I don't remember what's supposed to happen on birthdays.

Where will I be on my twelfth birthday? What will I do? Maybe there won't be any more birthdays. If there are birthdays, will I get a present? Perhaps on my twelfth birthday we will be free—but surely that is too much to hope for. What is "free," anyway? What does it mean? Where

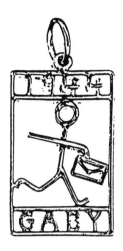

My eleventh birthday present:
the pendant showing me as an Ordonnanz (messenger).

will we go? What will we do? Is Hans going to be with us? Will we be going back to school?

I have so many questions, but there is no reason to ask Mami or
Papi because they don't know the answers, either. I say nothing, I
ask nothing. When they come back to the barracks after work, I tell
them of my unexpected birthday present, and I feel very guilty that
I didn't save any of the bread to share with them.

Then comes the second surprise of the day: Mami and Papi give
me a necklace with a pendant made of brass. The pendant shows a
girl running with one arm outstretched and a letter in her other
hand. Above the girl is the year, 1944, and below her the name by
which I was then called, Gaby. It was designed by my father's friend,
the Dutch artist Jo Spier, and cut out by my father's pharmacy assistant, the goldsmith.

I am delighted with the necklace, put it on immediately, and
wear it constantly from that day on. After that the day is finally
over, and I go to bed. I have grown up a little more and feel very
adult: now I am eleven.

Two Jobs

After a certain time, children from the age of ten also had to work in Theresienstadt. Therefore, I had to go every morning to the Magdeburg Barracks, where the administration would assign me to a job. I was assigned to be an *Ordonnanz*, a message carrier. There were many of us, naturally, but some of us were permanently assigned to a particular building. I was assigned to the *Siechenheim*, or home for the elderly and sick elderly. There I had to carry notes or oral messages within the *Siechenheim*, or I might be sent to another barracks with a message.

•

The *Siechenheim* has long, long rooms with many beds in which the sick cough, sneeze, moan, groan, and scream, and which have an indescribable smell made up of a mixture of overflowing outhouse, bad food, unwashed bodies, and putrefaction. Between the office, where I sit on a bench when I am not being sent somewhere, and the main hall, there is a small courtyard. It is bare of plants or other living things, with only one exception: an old man in a wheelchair. His body and limbs are deformed, and he shakes constantly. His head is like a skull and nods all the time. His face is yellowish. He beckons to me whenever I pass; he tries to smile at me and talk to me; but he frightens me to such an extent that I can still see him today as clearly as if it were yesterday. He pursues me in my dreams for many years afterward.

During my time as an *Ordonnanz*, I demonstrate again that I have learned my "lessons" very well. I am sent to the Hamburg Barracks to give a note to someone there. When I arrive at the room, a private room, I knock on the door and soon find out that no one is there. I open the door and enter to leave the note in a conspicuous place. As I leave I see a small wheelbarrow made of yellow copper. Quick as a magpie, I reach out, snatch it up, and put it in my pocket. On my way out I meet someone who is entering the room—its inhabitant? I greet him, he greets me; he sees the note, he thanks me, and I walk away. No one ever says anything about the wheelbarrow, and when, much later, I am asked where I got it, I answer that I traded something else to another child for it.

One day I am given a note to take to the "pharmacy." It does not have, as a real pharmacy would, jugs and bottles of interestingly colored liquid or jars and pots of strange-smelling salves. It's more like a sort of cave with shelves sparsely lined with medications the dead have left us. I go into this cave-like room where my father works and give the note to him. He reads it, then he writes an answer. That done, he turns to me and invites me to, *Sit down, sit down, talk to us for a while. You are not in such a hurry, are you?*

I look at him, scared to say yes and scared to say no. If I say no, I may hurt his feelings. If I say yes, I'll get back to work later than they think I should, and I'll get into trouble. Finally I make up my mind and answer, *No, Papi, I cannot. I have to go back to work.* Both my father and his assistant have a hard time controlling their laughter, but my father accepts my answer and lets me go.

When I get out of the pharmacy, I breathe a sigh of relief. At least the soldiers cannot shoot me for an infraction.

•

Eventually the *Ordonnanz* job ended. For a while I had no other, until the day when I received a notice that I was to come to the crematorium. Theresienstadt had no gas chambers, but the inmates died of starvation, a variety of diseases, or sometimes were tortured to death. Burial was out of the question; the ground was marshy and water seeped into the graves. Therefore all the dead were cremated.

•

The job I am called to do is given only to children, as far as I know, and consists of standing in a line with other children. We enter the crematorium; the entrance is a long, dark hall, and it's like entering into a rock. From there we form a long line. The first child in line hands cardboard boxes filled with ashes down the line of waiting hands. There is a certain rhythm to the work: we throw one box, turn around, stretch out our arms, catch the next box, turn again and throw it to the next child in line. Once in a while someone fails to catch a box, it falls to the floor, breaks open, and the ashes go flying. We amuse ourselves by looking at the names on the boxes to see whether we know the person whose ashes are inside. Now and then a child will call out:

There goes my uncle!

That was my friend!

Whether these comments are true, I don't know, but in order not to be different I also call out, *Hey, did you see that name? That's my grandmother!*

It wasn't though; my grandmother had died in Westerbork, so I couldn't possibly have found her ashes here in Theresienstadt.

We are "paid" for this job, since it isn't a regularly assigned one. At the end of the day we each receive a tiny bit of sausage. I want so much to take that bit of sausage to our room and share it with my parents, but I am too hungry; I can't hold out, and eat it on the way to our barracks.

•

I had this job twice, twice received the bit of sausage, and twice ate it on the way to the barracks. Years later, when I was already in my late forties, any time I remembered that job and that bit of sausage I still felt guilty that I had not saved it to share with my parents.

Theresienstadt crematorium.

I Am Ill Again

With the vastly overcrowded and filthy conditions in Theresienstadt, it was no wonder that various diseases made their regular rounds. Impetigo, severe jaundice, enteritis, dysentery, abdominal typhus, spotted typhus, various forms of tuberculosis were common, as were unusually severe forms of other diseases such as measles, scarlet fever, mumps, and sties on the eyes. Even the tiniest wounds became infected, festered, and suppurated.

•

In one of our games in the courtyard of the Hamburg Barracks, I try to run over the big pump stone in the center of of the yard. On the round stone is a round metal duct with a roof-shaped cover. I need to jump over it, but I don't jump high enough, stumble over it and fall full-length on the sharp cobble stones. For a moment I lie still; then I feel a deep, sharp pain in my knee. When I look, I see streams of blood, and I instantly begin to scream at full lung power.

Oooooohh! Ouch, ouch, ouch! Mami, help me! Mami! Mami! Mami! Ooouuuch, it hurts! MAMI!

Slowly I manage to get up, and with the help of my playmates I limp my way up the stairs to our room. On the stairs I keep feeling that the other children poke their fingers into my knee, but I daren't look. Tears stream down my face, my mouth is wide open, and I have lost the power even to utter a word; only inarticulate sounds come out. My mother has heard my screams and comes running to meet me. She takes one look at my leg and turns me around. We don't even go to our room, but go straight to the "clinic." This is a place I am much afraid of, because whatever they do there, it always hurts. I scream louder. A woman in a white smock or apron lifts me up on a table and cleans my leg, accompanied by still more screams from me. Then she puts a wad of cotton wool on it, binds a paper bandage around it of the same type we used in Westerbork, and finally my mother takes me back to our room. The leg continues to hurt, but by now I'm past the first shock and I don't say anything.

The next morning, though, when I get up to go to the washroom, I promptly fall over. My leg has gone stiff overnight. So back we go to the "clinic," where a man in a white smock—a doctor?—takes a look at the cotton wool and shakes his head.

Now, who put that on there? That has to come off! I'll need to clean it again and re-bandage it.

Already my tears begin to flow, but this time I make no sounds. It takes a long time to get the cotton wool off the wound; the doctor needs to soak it off.

That's quite a hole you have there, girl. How did you manage that? It's as big as a dime, and it goes all the way to the bone. I should suture it, but —turning to my mother—*we don't have the wherewithal. No thread, no needles, nothing. I'll just have to wrap it up and hope for the best.*

So that's what he does. Then we leave and go to our room. My leg gets stiffer and stiffer; pus saturates the paper bandage, and I develop a fever. But in a week or so, the fever leaves, my leg begins to limber up, and the hole begins to close. After several weeks I can walk again.

•

It was not until several years after the war that I knew just how lucky I had been. Somehow the infection had cleared up, and other than a dime-sized scar on my knee, I never had any residual effects from that fall.

Any time we got shots against diphtheria or other diseases, the place where the needle went into my arm or chest became infected and suppurated. In Theresienstadt this was normal, and took me a long time after the war was over to understand that getting inoculated does not automatically produce suppurating infections. However, I have never gotten over my fear of hypodermic needles.

One of the recurrent illnesses that befell me was a middle-ear infection. In the year and a half we spent in Theresienstadt, I had five or six of them.

•

On one occasion, when my ear hurts once again, my mother takes me to the *Poliklinik*, the clinic, where we wait and wait and wait. Finally we are called in, and Mami explains what is wrong with me while I sit with my hand clamped to my ear. It hurts badly; I keep thinking that maybe there is a tiny knife in my ear. That's how it feels. Mami and the doctor talk for a while, then he calls me over and looks into my ear. His face is very serious when he tells Mami to leave the room and wait outside, that he has to lance whatever is in the ear.

I don't know what "lance" means, but I'm about to find out. He tells me to sit on the nurse's lap, and I say indignantly, *Why? I'm a big girl. I don't have to sit on anyone's lap.* But he insists, and I climb onto her lap. She puts her arms around me, around my arms, and holds me very tightly. I protest, *I can't move!*, but it does no good, and nobody answers me. Then another nurse comes over to me and puts five little blobs of some sort of cream on my face, one on each cheek, one on my forehead, one on my chin, and one on the tip of my nose. A piece of gauze goes over that. The doctor tells me to count aloud backwards from ten to one. As soon as I start, the second nurse comes with a spray and sprays a foul-smelling liquid on my face.

I count from nine to eight and then I open my mouth wide and scream and scream and scream. The room begins to turn, I feel very strange, and I can't hear my own screams anymore. When I manage to open my eyes again, my throat is hoarse from my screams and I have a horrible taste in my mouth. I feel as though I'm going to be sick, but am not. The doctor goes to the door and lets Mami back in. He explains to her that I screamed because of the ether, that really, truly, I didn't feel what they did. That is true, but now I cannot stop crying.

Mami gives me a white woolen stocking cap (where did she get it?) that I have to wear on my head, pulled down over the sick ear to keep it warm, and then we go back to our room. She tucks me in bed and I finally fall asleep, exhausted and frightened. Eventually, after a long time, the ear heals—for now—and I am able to get about again.

My Nightgown and Other Clothes

Every time something like that happened, I had to stay in bed, of course. I suppose I must have brought a pair of pajamas with me when we were deported from Amsterdam, but they must have been too small for me by this time, because now I had a nightgown made of the same material used for bed sheets.

•

My mother is not a very good seamstress, and the nightgown does not fit very well. Worse by far, though, is its color. Only two colors are available for dying the material: either a bilious blue or a deep poisonous pink. Where the dye comes from, or who dyes the material, I don't know; but these are the only colors. My nightgown is the deep poisonous pink, a dreadful color! It's quite enough to make me sicker than I already am. Still, I have no choice. I must wear it, and there is no use in saying anything about it. When I am not too ill to do anything at all, I either read in bed or retreat into fantasy, into a better place. Of course, I do have to come back to *this* place, but at least for a little while I am out of the misery.

•

Now, in hindsight, it seems to me that both Hans and I transformed our reality into imagination and our fantasies into reality, thereby making the imagination bad and the reality good. It didn't change anything, of course, but it helped us to view the situation at a safe distance. It stayed that way after the war; whenever I felt bad about something, I simply slipped through the doorway into my "other world" until things either got better or I could face them.

Other than illness, my other problem in Theresienstadt was the cold. Theresienstadt is located in a basin, and its winters are extremely cold, its summers very hot. I don't remember ever feeling too hot, but I always felt cold. Today, when I think back, I still shiver; it seems to me that I was always cold. Of course, I didn't have many clothes—nobody did. With the abominable food—or rather, the lack of it—I didn't grow very fast, but I did grow a little, and slowly I had grown out of those clothes I had worn when we were first deported. True, I still had my purple knee-socks and some other things, but most of my clothes were either in rags or far too small. In order to acquire "new" clothes, we had to go the the *Magazin*, German for warehouse and used to mean "shop" in the camp. There we could "buy" clothes, sometimes—clothes left behind by people who had been sent on transport or clothes of people who had died. One of my most precious possessions until long after the war was a taffeta dress of lustrous red plaid that had been "bought" in this way. It had short sleeves and a billowing skirt. I thought it magnificent, and was heartbroken when I eventually grew out of it and had to give it away. Generally, though, I was dressed in dark blue shorts and, in summer, nothing else. I was supposed to wear my wooden *klompen*, but I often forgot and went barefoot. In winter I still wore the shorts or a skirt, and probably a blouse of some sort. I had no other stockings than the purple knee-highs to wear in my wooden shoes. I also had the loden coat I had inherited from my cousin and which kept some parts of me somewhat warm. But still I was always cold, terribly cold. It snowed in winter, and somehow I remember the sky as being always gray. Everything was gray: the sky, the streets, the barracks inside and out, people's faces, the food. They weren't gray in reality, but they were gray in *my* reality.

Whatever clothes we had, then, came from the *Magazin*. The

Nazis had printed and issued to us "ghetto money," paper money that was usable only in Theresienstadt. The unit of currency was called *Kronen*, crowns, and came in bills of various denominations: two crowns, ten crowns, fifty crowns, and so forth. On one side of the bills was a picture of Moses holding the tablets with the Ten Commandments, and the bill's value printed in a number. On the other side was the amount printed in letters, under which was the printed signature of the "Elder" of Theresienstadt, Jacob Edelstein. The "Elder" was a sort of governor, appointed by the Nazis and working under their orders. On the side with the picture of Moses there was also some text, which read: *"Wer diese Quittung verfaelscht oder nachmacht oder gefaelschte Quittungen in Verkehr bringt, wird strengstens bestraft."* ("Whoever falsifies this note, alters it fraudulently, or imitates it, or whoever puts false notes into circulation, will be severely punished.")

ABOVE AND OVERLEAF: *Theresienstadt money,*
in denominations of ten, two, and fifty crowns.

I Learn to Read German

Any kind of school, learning, or studying was of course strictly forbidden in Theresienstadt. In the "children's homes" the adults did teach the children clandestinely, but for the rest of us there were no educational opportunities. Yet I learned some things other than "organizing" and lying. Theresienstadt had a "library," consisting of books which inmates had left behind when going on transport or when they died. The books had been put into some order, and the inmates could go to the building where they were kept and borrow them. There were very few, if any, books in Dutch, the language in which I had learned to read; so if I wanted to read, I had to read in German. My parents had continued speaking German at home, both between themselves and to me, and although I generally answered them in Dutch, I did understand German and could speak it as well. But I had never learned to read or write German. Since I had learned to read in Dutch, I had learned only the Roman alphabet; the German books in the Theresienstadt library, however, were printed in gothic characters (Fraktur). Like it or not, I had to learn to decipher these if I wanted to read.

•

Mami, what does this say? I can't read it.

Yes, you can. Just figure it out from the meaning. You know what it's supposed to say.

No, Mami, please help me. It's difficult, and the letters all look alike.

Now, what letter do you suppose that is?

I think it's an "f." But that makes a word I don't know.

What word do you think it should be?

Should it be "Fenster" (window)?

Of course. See, you can read this. Just pretend the curls and little tails on the letters are not there and think of what makes sense in the sentence.

•

And so I did learn to read the Fraktur alphabet, by process of elimination. If it was not logical, it had to be wrong. Pretty soon I read it fluently.

I also learned to write in German, though I don't remember doing it very often. There was no need for it; I wasn't writing any letters or anything like that. Still I learned it somehow.

Mami Is in the Hospital

At some time during our imprisonment in Theresienstadt, my mother also fell ill and had to go to the hospital. Yes, Theresienstadt had a hospital. It had big rooms, with beds made up with real sheets and pillow cases. Too many patients were crowded in the rooms, true, but they were taken care of by real nurses and real doctors— inmates all—as far as these were able. Without real medications and without other necessary supplies, that care was always difficult. The hospital was located in the Hohenelbe Barracks, which was the central hospital. All sorts of sick people were there; there were departments for surgery, urology, internal medicine, and many others, including infectious diseases.

My mother was suffering from neuralgia in the face, just under the right eye. I don't know what the normal treatment for this is, but in Theresienstadt the only solution was to kill the nerve that caused this very painful disease. It was treated by injecting alcohol into the affected nerve, deadening it and thereby the pain; but it also pulled my mother's face to the right so that her mouth looked as though it were located in the middle of her right cheek. It stayed that way, crooked, for many months.

It was a miracle that my mother did not catch any infectious disease while she was in the Hohenelbe, since hospital patients were allowed to visit one another and so roamed freely throughout the barracks. In fact, it is a miracle that none of us ever caught anything like the typhus that was ever present in Theresienstadt; I think it must have been my parents' vigilance and insistence on as much cleanliness as possible which prevented us from having any kind of lice, which, after all, were the carriers of typhus and other diseases.

•

While Mami is in the hospital, Papi and I go to visit her.

What am I supposed to say? I don't know what to do. Is a hospital scary? Am I going to catch lice? Is Mami still hurting?

Papi tries to prepare me somewhat.

You mustn't be afraid of Mami, you know. She's going to look different. Her face isn't the way you're used to seeing it, because of the injection she got. She may not be in a very good mood because of all this. Don't mind what she says; she doesn't mean it, okay?

Well, that's not very reassuring! I try to walk more slowly and pull on Papi's hand. He won't let me, though, and anyway, Theresienstadt is so small that you always get where you're going very quickly. Before I expect it, we arrive at the Hohenelbe. Like the other barracks in Theresienstadt, it is a rather threatening build-ing; knowing that it is used as a hospital doesn't help at all. We walk through long halls until we come to a big room with too many beds. In one of them lies my mother. She is pale, paler than usual, and her hair is very dark against the pillow. Papi is right: she doesn't look like her usual self. She tries to smile at me, and all I want to do is run away. Her face is not right; it doesn't even look quite human anymore. It looks like the faces of the demons about which I have read so much in my books before the war!

Oh, no, that's not my mami! It can't be! She doesn't look at all like Mami. That is a stranger. Doesn't Papi notice it? It must be the wrong bed. What do I do now? And what do I say? My throat is very dry and my tongue is thick. I want out of here! I want to leave!

I suppose I must have finally stammered something; in any event, no one scolds me when Papi and I leave. After a few days my mother returns to the barracks and life goes on as before. But every once in a while, when I don't prepare myself before looking at my mother, I still get a shock when I see her face. Eventually I get used to it, and after a while I no longer notice it.

•

It took many years for my mother's face to go back to normal, and even after those years, when the weather was damp her mouth would pull somewhat to the right. But...the neuralgia never came back.

The Beautification

Theresienstadt was conceived by the Nazis as a "model ghetto," which would show the world that the Nazis might have relocated the Jews, but that the Jews didn't have it bad at all. The Nazis thought that if anyone saw this "ghetto," no further questions would be asked about any other "ghettos" or camps. In spring 1944, a rumor began to make the rounds that we could expect a visit of representatives from the International Red Cross. For that reason, to show Theresienstadt at its best and to make a good impression on the Red Cross representatives, the Nazis decided that the town had to be less crowded, that it should be cleaned up and had to be beautified.

The process began in May 1944. The first thing to do, of course, in order to have fewer "inhabitants" in Theresienstadt, was to send several transports to the East. In May the first one, consisting of 7,500 persons, left, followed in short order by two more of 2,500 persons each, including all of Theresienstadt's orphans and most of its tuberculosis patients, since neither of those categories of people fit in with the idea of a "model town." This having been done, all sorts of other embellishments began. The streets were repaired, street signs with real names like Seestrasse (Lake Street) were put up, the facades of the buildings were painted, signposts with small carved figures on them and words like "to the library" or "to the showers" were erected. The main square of the town, in front of the

Nazi headquarters, which had a cobblestone pavement, was ordered transformed—within one week—into a park with grass, gravel paths, benches, flower beds, and even a bandstand, painted bright yellow, for the Theresienstadt orchestra. Yes, there was a Theresienstadt orchestra! The instruments had been left by those who had been sent East, or had been acquired some other way. The musicians did not always have written scores, but they managed without. A band of forty musicians had to play in the bandstand three times a day, at least while the Red Cross representatives were there. Before that nobody was allowed to enter the park, on penalty of death.

The children acquired a playground—in which we were not allowed to play—with a glass-covered pavilion with rocking horses, swings, toys, and a paddling pool. On the interior walls the Dutch artist Jo (Josef) Spier had been forced to paint a mural with motifs after Noah and the Ark. Varnished beds for afternoon naps were also provided. The adults acquired a café on a terrace with parasols over the tables, at which they were forced to sit while the visitors were there and which they were not allowed to use at any other time. A community center was built, with a prayer hall, a library, and a stage. A "concert hall" was opened in which was installed a genuine Bechstein piano, sent from Prague. High-quality goods, such as clothes, lingerie, and meat products appeared in shop windows—but were, naturally, not for sale. The bank of the "Jewish Self-Government" was created and began to circulate the ghetto money described earlier. One of the existing buildings had the word "school" painted above the entrance—and a poster on the wall stating that the school was closed for vacation. Naturally it was not normally used; we children were not allowed any education, after all. A sports field was constructed on the ramparts around the town, complete with dressing rooms and showers. Eleven soccer teams had to compete there. The ground-floor rooms in the barracks were painted and nicely furnished so that the visitors could see through the windows how well we lived. Even a cemetery was opened, in spite of the fact that the dead were cremated. The graves were, of course, imitation graves.

The commission of the International Red Cross finally arrived on June 23, 1944. Obviously, what the commission saw and what really existed were two very different things. As far as I know today, it was never really established whether the members of the commission were taken in by all the falsifications, or whether they noticed that what they saw were really just make-believe "stage sets." In any event, the International Red Cross did nothing about either Theresienstadt, or any other concentration camp.[5]

The Film

Since the beautification of Theresienstadt had already taken place, the Nazis now decided to take advantage of it to make a propaganda film about their "model ghetto" to show the world—particularly the Germans—how good we Jews had it there in sharp contrast to the poor Germans who suffered so much in Germany! The idea for this came from S.S. General Hans Guenther, who was then the director of the Prague Central Office for Jewish Emigration. He ordered the film made and asked Mr. Peceny, head of the weekly newsreel "Aktualita" in Prague, to serve as production manager. Two professional camera men from the same organization were to do the actual filming; the prisoners of Theresienstadt were forced to do all the other work. The film was to be called *Der Fuehrer schenkt den Juden eine Stadt*, (*The Fuehrer Grants the Jews a City*). It was supposed to show Theresienstadt as it never was: the Jews living there, according to the film, "had no worries; they were parasites on society now as ever; they had in mind nothing but a life of luxury, pleasure, and sitting in cafés, while the poor Aryans bled to death, or at least worked themselves to death."[6]

In the summer of 1944, S.S. Hauptsturmfuehrer Karl Rahm, then commandant of Theresienstadt, ordered actor/director Kurt Gerron, well known in prewar Germany (he had appeared in the premiere of *The Threepenny Opera* in Berlin, as well as in the film *The Blue Angel*, and had been director of many films for the UFA in Germany) to prepare the film, write a script, and direct the film. When Gerron, who was horrified by the idea and didn't want to do this, asked the Council of Elders—the Jewish "self-government"—what to do, the council told him that there was no way to refuse the order. So Gerron wrote the script.[7] He had two main helpers in this task: Jo Spier, the talented Dutch artist previously mentioned, and Frantisek Zelenka, a Czech who had been a stage designer in Prague before the war. Filming began on August 16, 1944, and finished on the following September 11. During those twelve days, some 42,000 feet of film were shot.

The Making of the Film

The only fragment of the film which is still extant today consists of about 651 feet. As mentioned, the "actors" were we, the prisoners of Theresienstadt, who naturally did not want to do this but were forced to, just as much as Gerron, Spier, and Zelenka were. One of the documents in H.G. Adler's book *Die Verheimlichte Wahrheit* shows this in a note sent by Gerron on August 31, 1944, in which he said that he needed 3,000 spectators for a soccer game, preferably many young people and definitely no old people. If necessary, Gerron wrote, they would have to be "drummed up" in the barracks.[8]

Notifications were sent out to the prisoners to come to rehearsals; those who did not come voluntarily were forced, receiving warnings that they would be fetched if they did not come, and that they could expect severe punishment in case they were absent. Only prisoners who looked "typically Jewish" were supposed to be used; anyone who was blond was excluded. Everyone was also supposed to look healthy, and all the "actors" were professionally made up and coiffed. There were all sorts of scenes: prisoners receiving parcels at the post office (the film did not show that the parcels had to be given back immediately; the actors had to circle back behind the "post office" and hand their boxes back over), prisoners having coffee in the café, listening to a concert, and watching a diving competition in the swimming pool. Of course, there was no swimming pool in Theresienstadt, so this was filmed in the river Eger. The film did *not* show that the sides of the river were barricaded by S.S. men in boats, making very sure that no one escaped. An open-air music hall performance was filmed as well, in the Drabschitzer Kessel, a meadow outside Theresienstadt where 2,000 "spectators" were waiting. The film did *not* show that the meadow was in reality a swamp in which the "actors" stood up to their ankles in water—to remind them, no doubt, that they were not there for their pleasure. Equally *not* shown was the police cordon around the meadow. Toward the end of the film, scenes in the barracks were shown: women doing their hair and children playing. One of the women sitting on a bench, unsmiling and with a sad look in her eyes, is my mother, and I am one of the little girls sitting on a bench with my back to the table, staring at the camera without any expression.

Hans Hofer writes in his article "Der Film ueber Theresienstadt" ("The Film on Theresienstadt") in the book *Theresienstadt,* "One day the nightmare disappeared as quickly as it had appeared. The band was no longer allowed to play, no one was allowed to sit on the benches, dancing was prohibited and threatened with severe penalties and the general comfort which the film falsely showed gave way again to the grey routine of Theresienstadt, with dirt, hunger and diseases."[9] Adler speaks of the film both in his book *Theresienstadt 1941-1945: Das Antlitz einer Zwangsgemeinschaft* and in his other book *Die Verheimlichte Wahrheit: Theresienstaedter Dokumente.* In the first of these he says, "Of the true Theresienstadt, practically nothing was shown. It was a pure fable showing people how the most stupid Jew-hater might imagine Jews to be. Hardly any work was shown, just a few pictures of the building of the railway installation, a few workshops, and the 'agriculture,' which was not typical of the concentration camp. The misery, wretchedness, distress, and need were not shown."[10] Adler calls the film "...a ghostly satire as background to the abysmal demonic nature of concentration- and extermination camps,"[11] and speaks of "...this work of organized madness."[12]

A week or ten days after the film was finished, beginning September 20, 1944, rumors began to circulate about deportations, rumors which shortly turned out to be true. Since the 60,000 "extras" were no longer needed, all but 12,000 were "liquidated," sent to extermination camps, mostly to Auschwitz. Gerron and all his staff, with the exception of Jo Spier and Hans Hofer, were murdered in Auschwitz.

Eventually some music and a narration were added to the film. The final version was finished in March 1945 and copies were sent to Berlin. After that, nothing more was heard of it until 1965, when fragments of it were found in the archives of the Czech newsreel office.

I have no memory of the making of this film. All I remember is being dressed in a white blouse and a dark blue skirt with straps which crossed in the back, then came forward over my shoulders and were attached in front with white buttons. Where these clothes came from I have no idea; perhaps they were "lent" to me for the purpose of the filming; perhaps they came from the *Warenmagazin*, the "clothing store." In any event, it felt very strange to be dressed so formally; not only were they not my clothes, but my usual outfit in Theresienstadt consisted of the previously mentioned shorts and clogs. So I did not feel myself in the blouse and skirt.

When I finally watched the surviving fragment of the film in 1986, I recognized my mother and me in it. It came as a shock, and I could hardly believe what I saw. Yet I had always known of this film; my father spoke of it occasionally. Still, seeing my mother and me on film made the time in Theresienstadt very real.

After the Film

The transports on which people were sent to their deaths became known later as the "autumn transports." With so many prisoners gone, Theresienstadt seemed emptier than it had ever been, although it was still overcrowded. I, too, felt empty; my friend Hans and his whole family—mother, father, and brother—had been sent to Auschwitz. I did not know that then; I only knew that they were being sent "east," and both Hans and I knew that we would probably never see each other again, even though we didn't know exactly what would happen to them or where they were going. However, since to our knowledge, no one had ever come back to Theresienstadt from the East, we had few doubts about Hans' return.

•

The transports have to assemble in the courtyard of the Hamburg Barracks. My father has conceived the idea of going there with me. Perhaps we can say goodbye to Hans and his family. We approach slowly; we don't want to be caught up in this transport. People mill around in the courtyard, trying to stay with their families. The courtyard is filled with people: some sit on their little bit of luggage, perhaps to protect it from thieves or so as not to lose it; others try for a last-minute reprieve in order to stay in Theresienstadt; still others try to find their name on one of the "protected" lists. If they can find their names on one of these lists, they don't have to go on transport—at least not on this one. We all know that it is only a postponement of the inevitable, not a permanent reprieve, but any postponement helps. At least Theresienstadt is not the unknown.

I look around, shivering slightly. I am afraid, as afraid to stay here as to go where Hans is going, though I don't know exactly where that is.

I don't want to be here. I don't want to do this. Yes, I do, I want to say goodbye to Hans. But I don't want to get stuck here and have to go with them. I want to stay here, with Papi and Mami. Would it be very bad not to say goodbye? I guess so; I would like Hans to say goodbye to me if I were going on transport. So I'd better go. I wonder where "East" is. It's also called "Poland," but I don't know where that is, either. How will I know, afterwards in Amsterdam, if Hans comes back? Papi will know; I can ask him…later.

I feel very lonely and alone after Hans is gone. I have no other real friends in Theresienstadt, nor do I make any from that day on. Of course, I do talk to other children; I know many others, but they are not friends like Hans. Being alone again thus weighs heavily on me. I mope around, with no friends and nothing to do outside of work, and with the idea foremost in my mind that any day now we, too, will be sent on transport and that my days are numbered. I never do ask either my mother or my father where or what "Poland" or "the East" is; somehow I know enough not to ask. I continue with my work, and the days pass one after the other and each as gray as the one before.

One day a change occurs. Along with the adults, many of the children are gone now too. We remaining children have no more assigned jobs; we have to help wherever help is needed. In November I receive one of the official notices with which everything is always announced in Theresienstadt. Typed and signed by the "Elder of the Jews," they tell people where to go and what to do. My note tells me—in German, which is the official camp language—that I have to go help gather chestnuts. The following is the text of the note, with its translation.

DU HAST ZUM KASTANIENSAMMELN ANZUTRETEN[13]

Namen: Silten, Ruth   XXIV/2-631   Jg 1933

Ubikation: Langestr. 5/228

Du hast im Auftrage der Dienstelle morgen, Donnerstag, den 9.11.44, um 7.30 Uhr frueh in der Landwirtschaft, Seestr. 3, zum Kastaniensammeln anzutreten.

Kinder, die ohne Bewilligung der Arbeitszentrale in Betrieben aushilfsweise arbeiten, sind von dieser Aufforderung nicht entbunden und haben daher anzutreten.

Theresienstadt, am 8.11.1944

Fuersorge,

YOU MUST REPORT FOR DUTY GATHERING CHESTNUTS

Names: Silten, Ruth   XXIV/2-631   Age group 1933

Domicile: Langestrasse 5/228

By order of the office, you must report for duty tomorrow, Thursday, November 9, 1944, at 7:30 A.M., in the agriculture office at 3 Seestrasse, for the gathering of chestnuts.

Children working temporarily in workshops without authorization from the work headquarters are not exempt from this order and must therefore report for duty.

Theresienstadt, November 8, 1944

(signed): Youth Welfare Service

My first name is indeed Ruth; as such it was used for official purposes, even though I was never called by it. The number XXIV/2-631 was my transport number, always used in Theresienstadt as an identification number. The original document was given by my father to Dr. H.G. Adler who shows it in his book *Die Verheimlichte Wahrheit* on page 193. The chestnuts were horse chestnuts and were to be used as feed for animals.

In November it was already bitterly cold; and even though we had no heating in our rooms, it was still warmer there than outside.

Winter clothes I had none, having either grown out of them or never having had any with me. After all, we had originally been deported in June; perhaps no one had thought that we would be in a concentration camp for such a long time. I still wore the coat I had taken with me to Westerbork; but that was a year and a half ago, and although I had not grown much, still the coat had become too short, would no longer close, and had sleeves which no longer reached to my wrists. Stockings or gloves I had none. So it was with great reluctance that I went to where I was called, but I had no choice. Like it or not, I went to gather chestnuts.

I have no memory of any trees in Theresienstadt, chestnut or otherwise. Either there really were none, or my memory has gone blank. Nor do I remember *where* we went to gather these chestnuts, nor *how* we gathered them. Did we gather those which had already fallen off the trees? Did we perhaps try to break them loose from the branches by using sticks or stones? What did we put them in? I have no answers to these questions. Did I do this job one day? Or did it last several days? There is no answer to those questions either. The job was there; it needed doing; along with other children, I was called to do it, and I did it. That's all I know.

Tommy

Tommy was one of the other children with whom I was friendly in Theresienstadt. I don't remember actually playing with him; rather, we used to have occasional conversations. He was the son of one of my father's friends, one of three children. His brother and sister were older than he, and therefore "much too old" to occupy themselves with either of us. I thought then that Tommy was about two or three years older than I, and felt very flattered that an almost-grown-up like him would not think it below his dignity to talk to such a "baby" as I was. One conversation with Tommy stands out particularly. We are in the middle of town, walking along what used to be the cobblestoned central square which has now been changed into a park. It has a large plot of grass with bushes of some sort of flowers which I don't recognize and can't name. We stop and look at it all; we haven't seen grass for such a long time. This sets us to thinking of the time before the war, when we could still go to the city parks to play. We didn't know each other then, but it turns out that both of us played with marbles and played ball games, hop-scotch, and other games. Both of us have tried to make a top spin in the park; both of us have found out that tops don't spin well on gravel or grass.

Tommy tells me he used to have a bicycle.

It was black, and I had learned how to ride it. I didn't even need blocks on the pedals to be able to reach them. I'm taller than you, that's why. It was shiny when I got it, too, and the seat was real comfortable. I had to learn to swing my leg over the seat, because boys' bicycles are different from girls' bikes; they have a straight bar across from the seat to the steering column. Girls' bikes have a short of U-shaped bar; that's for your dresses, I guess. Besides, boys are different from girls—so we have to have different bikes, too!

I am somewhat envious because I have never owned a bicycle and have never learned how to ride one. I probably won't ever have one now and will never learn how to ride one, I think. I regret that because Tommy says that it's very easy and lots of fun. He learned it in no time at all. After this most important conversation, we each go to our own quarters.

•

After liberation, I never saw Tommy again. Eventually, many, many years later, I learned that he and his family, all of whom survived, had emigrated to the United States. Still, I had no idea what had become of him or his family. Then one day I saw a book in a children's bookstore written by someone with the same last name as Tommy. The style of the drawings also looked very familiar. I wrote to the author of the book, explained who I was, and asked whether by any chance he was the son of my father's friend. If so, I wrote, I would be grateful for some information about his brother, my old friend Tommy. I received an answer by return mail, including the address of Tommy—meanwhile grown into "Tom." Tom and I were thus able to catch up somewhat on old times, whereby it turned out that he and I are just about of an age. Tom does not remember this bicycle conversation, and I don't really know why I do; but somehow the idea of owning and being able to ride a bicycle must have been very important to my eleven-year-old self.

Winter 1944

Slowly the autumn and winter of 1944 pass. It is bitterly, bitterly cold, both inside the barracks and outside, and there is snow on the ground. The grayness of Theresienstadt seems to become grayer and grayer; the mud and dirt, which suck my wooden clogs off my feet, seem to become thicker and stickier; the many sick and the many dead, the ever-present fear which I cannot always suppress, the gnawing hunger which, as hard as I try, I cannot ignore all the time—all do their part to make this time even more difficult. I also feel another kind of hunger, non-physical, which I cannot identify.

I become more and more withdrawn. I do my various jobs—cleaning, fetching food, mending stockings—without talking much or at all. Mostly I just look at the adults around me, observing how they too become grayer and grayer, thinner and thinner. They seem to dissolve into wisps of smoke—talking, moving smoke, smoke with arms and legs like ghosts—but not real people. I do not feel real anymore either. I have a pain inside of me which has become part of me and without which I don't know how to exist. Most of the time I'm not sure I exist at all. Probably I am not real anymore. Yes, I can see myself; I can feel it if I pinch myself; but even that sort of pain is not real. My imagination has died; I can no longer imagine what life was like "before," how I used to be, what I used to do, where I used to go. I can no longer think of what I would do if.... What if...? There is no "What if?" There is only "Now"—and the *now* isn't real. It is an existence between two worlds, the real and the unreal. The unreal becomes more and more real and more solid every day, and every day I become more of a shell with a very hidden core.

•

At the end of the war, and for a very long time thereafter, my core was hidden so deeply that even I did not know that it was hidden, but thought I had none. That seemed quite normal to me; as far as I knew everybody was like that.

•

With the spring of 1945, another disaster arrives. More and more people fall ill. Finally their disease is diagnosed as spotted typhus, an extremely virulent and infectious type of typhus, spread by body lice. We call them "clothes lice" because that is where we find them, in our clothes. There is nothing that anyone can do, naturally, with the exception of isolating the sick. However, in the overcrowded conditions in which we exist, even isolation does not help much. In the end, twenty-five percent of Theresienstadt's inmates die of this epidemic.[14]

In the middle of all this, we begin to hear odd noises. At least, they are odd noises to me; I have no idea what is going on. I hear loud explosions; I don't know what they are, and actually I don't care. On May 5, 1945, the S.S. leaves Theresienstadt.[15] I have no personal memory of this; the numbness and emptiness have done their jobs too well. Through May 6 and 7 there are more noises; later I find out they are cannon shots. There are some explosions in Theresienstadt. All of a sudden we children are not allowed to go out on the street. It no longer matters; we may live or we may die, but we have few or no feelings either way.

In the evening of May 7, 1945, the first Russian troops enter the camp.[16] When they march in I stand by the fence near the railroad tracks and watch. I suppose they are to march in proper rows, but they must be tired because they come in singly and in small groups.

They don't sing, they don't talk, they are really rather quiet. But...they wear boots, just like the Nazis. So, to me, it makes little difference that they do not wear the same uniform; any soldier is like any other soldier, in my eleven-year-old view, and they are all bad news. No good can come from this as far as I am concerned.

The Russians Are There

By the time the Russians marched in, we had had to move again from one of the many big barracks to a house, which was probably a private house before the war. Here my parents and I had one small room together. For the first time in two years we also each had our own single bed instead of bunk beds—a very strange experience for me. It was next to this house that the railroad tracks ran, and it was from the fence next to this house that I watched the Russians arrive. We had already been in this room for a little while when that happened; other than the fact that the house was a house and not a barracks, nothing else was different. We still had all the vermin to deal with as we had had in the big barracks.

•

One night I wake up in the middle of the night, as I do so often these days. I see Papi sitting straight upright in bed, a pair of pincers in one hand and a glass of water in the other. I know that he is trying to catch bedbugs. They come out when the light is on, so we never turn it off. Instead we wrap my dark blue cardigan around the lamp; then the room is in semidarkness. The wooden beds, the straw-sack mattresses and pillows, everything crawls with bedbugs. I think they look like the Russian army coming in; they seem to walk the same way: slowly and in disorderly rows. I have learned from the beginning to catch the bedbugs with my hands and kill them with my fingers; Papi is much more fastidious and catches them with a small pair of pincers which he has found who knows where. Once he has caught one, he drowns it in a glass of water. The lamp throws his shadow on the wall; he seems like one of the giants in prewar fairy tales, so tall and thin is he. When I wake in the night and see his long-drawn shadow, I figure all is normal. I can then try to go back to sleep.

•

One morning I awoke and found my father very agitated, pacing the room and more nervous than usual. He told us that he had been awakened by a noise in the night, a noise coming from the window. He sat up in bed to see what was happening; his shadow played on the wall, as always, and a soldier, who was in the process of climbing through the window into our room, took one look at the shadow and disappeared, frightened off by the sight of what must have seemed to him an enormous man. The soldier was one of the liberating Russian troops; had he not been frightened off, who knows what would have happened to us? At the very least my mother and I would no doubt have been raped; many women and girls were raped by the Russians once they had "settled in."

•

It makes me think back to the day the Russians arrived. I stare at them as they walk slowly into the camp. I have no feelings about them, as I have none about anything else. Certainly I feel no jubilation. Perhaps the adults know that we are being liberated, that the war is over. I am still eleven; I know no such thing.

More soldiers coming in? I thought they were leaving. At least, some of them left. These look different, though, I think. Or are they? They wear uniforms, too, and boots, like the Nazis; they can't be very different. After all, a soldier is a soldier. What will they do to us, I wonder? How much longer is this going to last? What do they all want from us? I'm hungry; do they bring any food? Will we get any more? No, they don't look as though they have any. I'm cold; I want to go inside!

And I go into the house.

Over the next few days, however, I do begin to realize that these soldiers are not Nazis. Still, in my view a soldier is not to be trusted; they may not be Nazis, but that doesn't mean anything. And indeed, nothing much different happens. We do not receive any more food; we are not allowed to leave Theresienstadt. As far as I am concerned, nothing has changed.

My Twelfth Birthday

A few weeks after the Russians "liberate" us, I turn twelve years old. This time, when I wake up in the morning I have forgotten that it is my birthday; it is simply a day like any other. We are still in Theresienstadt, the soldiers are still with us, I am still hungry, I am still cold and people around me are still dying. Nevertheless, Mami and Papi greet me once again with *Happy birthday!* And once again I am polite and say *Thank you.* I get up, wash, get dressed. There is a small piece of bread for breakfast. Afterwards Mami gives me a small parcel. I open it and find a necklace which, once again, my father's colleague the goldsmith-pharmacy assistant has made for me. This time it is the coat of arms of Theresienstadt: a wall with two towers on it, between which is a lion. Like the first necklace, this too is made of brass. In my eyes it might as well be gold; it shines and sparkles, and I am very happy with it. I put it around my neck right away.

Then Papi gives me another small parcel. This one turns out to hold twelve squares of *Traubenzucker*, grape sugar or glucose, one square for each of my years. Somehow he has found these in the pharmacy, or perhaps they have been sent there with other "medications." I assume he "organized" them; I doubt very much that he asked anyone for permission to take them for his daughter. Each square is pure white, brilliantly white, and individually wrapped in lovely, colorful paper.

My twelfth birthday present: the pendant showing the
coat of arms of Theresienstadt.

I think it would be a pity to eat them, they look so pretty. Still, they are very tempting, and I am still so very hungry. Maybe I could try just one? I unwrap one very slowly and take a tiny bite. I am very surprised: it is sweet! The sweetness floods my mouth. I haven't ever tasted anything like that, I think. I take a second bite and the miracle repeats itself. Much too quickly the first square is gone. Should I eat another one? I try very hard not to eat another right away, but I cannot withstand the temptation. All too soon the second one is gone as well, and then the third and the fourth. Then I have to stop; I am still hungry, and they still produce that wonderful sweet miracle—but now I am also sick to my stomach. It was worth it, though!

Return to Holland

After the typhus epidemic was more or less under control, people began to leave Theresienstadt. The first to go were the Czechs; I suppose it was easier for them to go home. They spoke Czech, they were in their own country, they might have been able to hitch a ride if any cars were on the roads at all, or catch a train if those were running and if the rails had not been blown up. They might even still have family left in the places from which they had come.

The next to go were the Danes. There were very few of them in Theresienstadt, and the Swedish Red Cross came in buses to pick them up and take them home to Denmark.

For the rest of us, transportation had to be provided. How this was accomplished, I have no idea; but a day finally came in June when we also left. My parents and I, along with the other Dutch, somehow got to Pilsen—also in Czechoslovakia—which, before the war, had been famous for the beer brewed there. Once again we were quartered in a big building, in big rooms—but in individual beds with clean white sheets. Later it turned out that this place was the local insane asylum. In order to make room for us, the patients had been crowded together in another part of the building. We were more or less able to to go where we wanted, although the townspeople stared at us when we walked through the town. There must have been transports from other camps as well, because we met friends of my parents who had not come with us from

Theresienstadt. The most important part for me was that there was a garden with a very tall old tree with enormous branches, some of which were quite close to the ground.

•

How wonderful! I can climb up and hide between the branches and the leaves. Nobody will find me if I just sit quietly on a branch. I will be safe there.

Hiding places are very important to me; I must have a place where no one can find me. And every afternoon when I receive a slice of bread—with sugar!—I take it, climb up into the branches, sit between the leaves and eat my bread in peace, secure in the knowledge that nobody knows I'm up there, and so nobody can come and take my bread away from me.

We stay in Pilsen for a week, and I don't have to do any work. I can hardly believe it, and spend much time in "my" tree so that I cannot be found and given something to do after all. After a week the three of us and some other Dutch people find ourselves on a big field. The adults are looking up into the sky.

What are they waiting for? What are they looking at? There is nothing there. There aren't even any clouds. We have our rucksacks, but there are no trains here. They couldn't run here, there are no rails. So what are we doing here? Are we going to have to walk home? Wait...there is a noise. Something is glittering in the sky. It's coming closer; it's very noisy.

And then the airplane lands. Papi takes me by the hand and walks toward the airplane. He helps Mami and me climb inside. Inside there are long benches along the walls, and there are holes closed with a sort of rubber stopper in the windows. We all sit on the benches, and the airplane leaves. I want to ask questions, but I've learned over the last few years that it is usually better not to ask anything, so I don't. Anyway, it's much too noisy to talk; the adults try but have to give up, because nobody can hear anybody else. After what seems a very long time, the airplane lands again and we all get out, stiff and sore. The noise continues in my ears long after we are not even near the airplane anymore. To my surprise, we hear Dutch spoken around us. We are back in Holland.

•

In later years I learned that the airplane in question was an army transport plane; but no one ever explained to me what the holes with stoppers in the windows were for. Could they have been for guns?

Eindhoven

We have landed in the city of Eindhoven, famous before and after the war because it is the home of the Phillips electronics factories. Every one around us speaks Dutch. How much softer it sounds to my ears than German! And it's much prettier! We walk from the airplane to the Phillips factories, which are now empty, and where we will be quartered until it has been decided what's to be done with us, whether we have a place to go to or not. We enter and see an enormous room with rows and rows of bright red mattresses on the floor. Real mattresses, not straw sacks! They are soft, and I can even bounce on them a little. We each get a whole mattress for ourselves, and we are not separated. As we go in a man touches me on the arm and says in Dutch, *Wacht eventjes, wait a minute. I have something for you.*

He hands me a small square of something brown. He looks at me, full of expectation. I look up at him, then down at the brown square. I say nothing.

Aren't you going to eat it? he asks, somewhat surprised. I look at him in horror, my stomach already beginning to contract as I answer, *I can't eat soap! I can't, I really can't!*

It takes a long time before I believe Mami's explanation that this really, honestly is not soap. It is chocolate, and it tastes good. But I cannot bring myself to try it right away. When I do, though, I like it very much.

•

We stayed in Eindhoven also for about a week. I remember it as a week full of sunshine—and perhaps it was. In June, even Holland has sunny days. But even if the days were cloudy, they certainly seemed sunny to me.

Return to Amsterdam

After about a week, one day a truck arrives. Not the kind in which we had been taken away a lifetime ago, but a regular truck with an open back. Where did the gasoline come from? Who paid for it? I don't know, not even today. The liberating army? It is certainly possible.

A number of people besides us climb into the truck, and off we go. It is a long, dusty, hot ride through Holland's countryside, and I enjoy the sun, the wind, and the flowers of the fields through which we ride. Nobody speaks much; perhaps we are all too emotional, too exhausted, too weak or too happy to be back in Holland. Every so often the truck stops; some people climb off, collect what luggage they have—it isn't much—and set off on foot in the direction of a town or village where maybe they have family or where they think they can find a place to stay. Wherever someone gets off we all wave and look after the departing people for as long as we can see them. The truck remains stopped every time until the people have disappeared from sight. Then we continue on our way. What way? I don't know and haven't asked. I don't know where we're going and don't much care. We are no longer in Theresienstadt, we are back in Holland; that's all that matters.

Toward late afternoon the truck, now half empty, arrives in Amsterdam. Once again we are driven to the Central Station. Once again we wait. Once again there are lists of names; there is a

Gabriele upon return to Amsterdam in June of 1945.
This was the I.D. photo taken at the Central Station when we came back.

medical examination and a disinfection station where we are powdered with DDT. A photographer is on hand to take pictures for identification cards which are made on the spot. Once again we wait in line. Finally, when it is our turn, the man who is registering people asks my father whether we have any place to go. Of course, my father says no. The man, however, continues to look on his list, then looks up in surprise and tells my father that we certainly do have a place to go. It turns out that as soon as the war was over, our prewar upstairs neighbors, Carla's family, had put their name on all sorts of lists, saying that as soon as we came back we must come and stay with them.

Somehow my father manages to hire a man with a bakery tricycle who is willing to load up our luggage and take us to Noorder Amstellaan. Several times the man asks me if I want to ride on top of the luggage in his tricycle; several times I answer no, for fear that he may ride away with me and I will be separated from my parents. After a forty-five-minute walk we finally come to the house, ring the bell, and are welcomed quite literally with open arms and long, warm hugs. My friend Carla is not at home; all Amsterdam, probably all Holland, is celebrating the end of the war and the occupation, and she is gone as well. Her father, Oom Wim, Uncle Wim, knows where she is likely to be; he takes me by the hand and draws me back into the street. Sure enough, within a very short time we find Carla and another neighbor girl, Anneke, and once again I am welcomed with open arms and long, warm hugs. *How was it in the camp?* Carla asks, but all I can do is just shrug my shoulders.

After the War

We stayed with our neighbors for a long time, probably at least a year. The winter of 1944-1945 was terrible in Holland. It was one of the coldest winters on record, and there was no fuel for heating. The streets were denuded of trees, the parks had lost their trees and bushes. People used broken-up furniture and anything else that would burn in their stoves to have at least a little heat. During this last war winter, the Germans sent as much food as possible to Germany, with the result that practically nothing was left for the Dutch. That winter has gone down in history as the *Hungerwinter*, when people died in the street of starvation, when they ate not only their cats and dogs, but also whatever rats and mice they could catch. They ate tulip bulbs cooked in various ways: tulip bulb meatloaf, tulip bulb stew, tulip bulb cakes. When at last the liberators came and brought with them powdered eggs, powdered milk, chocolate and all sorts of food, the Dutch were finally saved from total starvation. We did have rationing after the war, in fact for many years after the war, but nothing much was available. Sure, we had coupons for meat and eggs; but we couldn't buy any, for there weren't any to buy. Under those circumstances, when a family already has two children; then to take in another starving family of three, one of whom is a child, is nothing less than heroic. Yet that is what Carla's family did. Somehow they stretched what food there was; somehow they made it serve seven instead of four. Somehow they fed all of us.

Carla's family also reported to the police the woman who was in our former apartment and who was a member of the Nationaal Socialistische Bond, the Dutch Nazi party, and a collaborator. She was taken to prison, and we were able to rent the same apartment we had before the war.

Eventually, in August 1945, elementary school started again, and I had to go back to school. At first I was afraid; I had missed two years, after all. I soon found out, however, that everyone was in the same boat. The children in my fifth-grade class ranged in age from about eleven to about sixteen years of age, having also missed school because of being in hiding or in concentration camps or for various other reasons. Over the next few years I tried hard to catch up; I was able to pass from one grade to the next without having to re-peat any.

Slowly but surely life returned to normal, especially after all three of us were once again in our own apartment. Normal? No, not really normal. Too many people had "not come back"—i.e., had not survived; too many scars, both physical and psychic, remained—and remain even today. Too many fears remained and remain. Too many memories live within us. Too many ghosts surround us. But as my friend Carla said in one of her recent letters, *You came back. True, you came back without Omi, but you came back. How on earth was all this possible?*

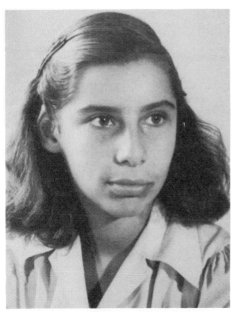

ABOVE: *Gabriele in 1947 at age 14*
BELOW: *My parents in the mid-fifties.*
My mother was about forty-six years old; my father was about fifty-one.

Epilogue

At this writing it is fifty years later, fifty years after the war, fifty years since all this happened. Why did I wait fifty years to write it all down? Why now, why not before?

Like many survivors, both adult and Child Survivors, I had to keep silence for all these years. It was simply impossible to talk about these things; we could not speak about our experiences, and people did not want to hear about them. In addition, I, like so many other children, was not allowed to speak out, but was told that I could not possibly have understood anything, that I could not possibly have suffered because, after all, I was only a child. The following poem, SURVIVOR'S SHEMA, which I wrote in November 1990, will perhaps explain best what happened to me, to us children, after the war was "over."

The *Shema* is the watchword of the Jewish faith, and that portion which I have reinterpreted in this poem reads, in English, in part, as follows: "Hear, O Israel, Adonai is our God, Adonai is One! You shall love the Lord your God with all your heart and with all your soul and with all your might. Set these words, which I command you this day, upon your heart. Teach them faithfully to your children; speak of them in your home and on your way; when you lie down and when you rise up. Bind them as a sign upon your hand; let them be a symbol before your eyes; inscribe them on the doorposts of your house, and on your gates. Be mindful of all my Mitzvot and do them: so shall you consecrate yourselves to your God."

SURVIVOR'S SHEMA

God said: "Let there be light,"
and there was light.
God saw that the light was good,
and God separated the light
from the darkness.

The Fuehrer said: "Let darkness reign,"
and darkness reigned.
He saw that the darkness served his purpose,
and he tried to banish the light
for all time.

Though we were children,
yet, in order to survive,
we were determined to resist,
with all our heart,
with all our soul,
with all our mind,
and all our might,
that force of darkness.

We carry in our hearts
a wound which does not heal,
which pains us still
when we lie down
and when we rise up.
We teach our pain to our children,
we speak of it in our homes,
it is inscribed upon the gates
of our memories.

It is a brand so searing
that it smoldered for forty years;
we dared not scream
·lest our scream
reverberate throughout the world
for forty days and forty nights.
The echo would rupture the world.

Our eyes have seen such horrors
that they have gone purblind.
We repressed our tears
for forty years;
we dared not cry
lest we shed tears
for forty days and forty nights.
The flood would drown the world.

Our minds are a conflagration of rage
burning for forty years—
our primary emotion—
a rage so great
we dare not lose our temper
lest we burn without restraint
for forty days and forty nights.
The blaze would shatter the world.

Our voices were silent
for forty years—
our silence was rewarded:
with life, during the war
with praise, after the war,
since we did not "bother" people
with our stories.

For forty years
we kept a silence so profound
that, even today, we dare hardly speak
lest our words pour forth
for forty days and forty nights.
The lament would deafen the world.

No matter what age we reach,
we will always be children:
the children of the Holocaust,
forged in flames,
tempered in tears,
hardened in pain,
yet now seeking justice
rather than vengeance.

Let the Holocaust be
a symbol before our eyes
of such darkness as must never be repeated;
let our tattooed numbers be
a sign upon our arms
of such evil as must never happen again;
so let us consecrate ourselves
to bearing witness,
from generation to generation,
so that no one will ever forget.

What Happened to Whom?

My Immediate Family

Gertrud Teppich, my maternal grandmother, committed suicide in November 1942, when she was on the point of being deported to Auschwitz.

Ernst Silten, my paternal grandfather, committed suicide in March 1943, when the Nazis were knocking on his door to deport him to Auschwitz.

Marta Silten, my paternal grandmother, committed suicide in July 1943 in the concentration camp Westerbork (Holland), when her name appeared on a list of people to be deported to Auschwitz.

Fritz Silten, my father, survived Westerbork and Theresienstadt. He died in November 1980.

Ilse Teppich-Silten, my mother, survived Westerbork and Theresienstadt. She died in February 1977.

Ursula Teppich, my aunt, my mother's sister, went to Switzerland in 1938 and lived there for the rest of her life. She died in May 1990.

Heinz (Henry) Silten, my uncle, my father's brother, went to England in the mid-thirties and lived there for the rest of his life. He died in March 1953.

R. Gabriele S. Silten, author of this book, survived Westerbork and Theresienstadt. I finished school after the war, went to high school in Amsterdam (Holland) and came to the USA in 1959, where I have lived since.

Other Family, Friends, and Acquaintances

Irene (Reni) and Werner, my cousins, survived Westerbork and Bergen-Belsen. They came to the USA and have lived here since after the war.

Carla, my upstairs neighbor and best friend, as well as her sister **Willy** and their parents, **Tante Trien** and **Oom Wim,** survived the war in Amsterdam. Tante Trien and Oom Wim have died, but Carla and her sister live in Holland today.

Mrs. Dornfeld and her daughter **Ellen:** I do not know their fate.

Hans, my only friend in Theresienstadt, and his brother **Werner,** as well as their parents **Eduard** and **Susanne,** were deported to Auschwitz in November 1944 and gassed there on arrival.

Max, my friend from across the street with whom I shared a schoolbench, went into hiding with his parents. He survived the war and came to the USA, where he lives today. He began searching for me in the eighties and finally tracked me down in December of 1987. We have since met again, are in regular contact, and are, once again (or perhaps still) friends.

Peggy, my girlfriend in elementary school, went into hiding with her aunt and uncle. They survived. I met Peggy again in high school, but after that we lost touch.

Tommy, now Tom, the son of my father's friend and one of the children with whom I was friendly in Theresienstadt, survived with his brother and sister and their parents. They came to the USA and have lived here since after the war.

Werner, my friend in Westerbork (neither my cousin nor Hans' brother, only the same name): I do not know his fate.

Kurt Gerron, actor and director of films in Germany, was deported to Auschwitz after the film "Der Fuehrer schenkt den Juden eine Stadt" was finished. He was murdered there.

Kurt Singer, my father's friend, was murdered by the Nazis.

Jo Spier, my father's friend, survived and came to the USA. He died in the seventies.

Glossary

Aap (Dutch) Monkey

"Achtung! Vorsicht! Durchgasung mit GIFTGAS! Lebensgefahr—Zutritt strengstens verboten!" (German) "Attention! Caution! Gassing with POISON GAS! Danger of death—entry strictly forbidden!"

Apenspel (Dutch) Monkey game; the name Carla and I gave to the game we played

Apotheke (German) Pharmacy

Appellplatz (German) roll-call place

Autoped (Dutch) Scooter

Bos (Dutch) Wood, forest

Buchtel (German?) A bakery item between a biscuit and a sweet roll.

Centraal Station (Dutch) Central (railway) Station (in Amsterdam)

Der Fuehrer schenkt den Juden eine Stadt (German) *The Fuehrer Grants the Jews a City*, title of the propaganda film made by the Nazis in Theresienstadt

Etensdrager (Dutch) Food carrier, a wooden tray with handle, on which to carry one's food to the barracks

Fenster (German) Window

Glimmer (German) Mica

Groene (Dutch) Green; the Nazis, who wore green uniforms

Harlekijntje (Dutch) Little Harlequin; a series of Dutch children's books recounting the adventures of Little Harlequin

Hollandsche Schouwburg (Dutch, old spelling) Dutch National Theater

Jet (Dutch) Feminine name

Joodsche Raad (Dutch, old spelling) Jewish Council, a group of Jews formed by order of the Nazis to carry out Nazi orders; euphemistically called Jewish self-government

Joodsche Schouwburg (Dutch, old spelling) Jewish Theater; wartime name of the National Theater

Joodsche Weekblad (Dutch, old spelling) Jewish Weekly, a newspaper

Kinderheim (German) Children's home

Kinderkamer (Dutch) Child's (or children's) room

Klomp, pl. **klompen** (Dutch) Dutch wooden shoes; clogs

Knie (Dutch) Knee; also the proper name Knie, the name of a circus family

Knijpkat (Dutch) A flashlight operated by a small dynamo; lit. squeeze-cat

Krone, pl. **Kronen** (German) Crown(s), the monetary unit used in Theresienstadt

Leesplankje (Dutch) The wooden terraced board on which we learned to read

Levenslicht (Dutch) Light of life; thick birthday candle marked off in twenty-one sections, one for each year

Lirum, Larum, Loeffelstiel; kleine Kinder fragen viel (German) An expression used by mothers when they no longer wish to answer questions; in English, something like Crickety, crackety, cooking pot; little children ask a lot (free translation)

Luftseife (German) Air soap, which lost two thirds of its volume as soon as it was held under water (camp jargon)

Magazin (German) Warehouse; in Theresienstadt, a store where one could buy clothes, etc.

Mami (Dutch and German) Mommy

Mevrouw (Dutch) Mrs.

Mies (Dutch) Feminine name

Mof, pl. **Moffen** (Dutch) Derogatory name for Germans

Nationaal Socialistische Beweging (Dutch) National Socialist Movement; the Dutch Nazi party

Nesthaeckchen (German) or **Benjaminnetje** (Dutch) Benjamin; figuratively, the youngest of the family; from a series of German/Dutch children's books recounting the adventures of Benjaminnetje

Nog drie minuten, dames (Dutch) three more minutes, ladies.

Noot (Dutch) Nut

Omi (German) Grandma

Onderduiken (Dutch) War jargon, literally to dive under; to go into hiding

Oom (Dutch) Uncle

Opa (German and Dutch) Grandpa

Opklapbed (Dutch) Bed that folds up into the wall; fold-away bed

Oppakken (Dutch) War jargon meaning to pick up, round up, arrest

Ordonnanz (German) Orderly; a messenger in a concentration camp (camp jargon)

Organize (English) To steal (camp jargon)

Overvalwagen (Dutch) Police assault van; in wartime, army trucks in which Jews were rounded up

Papi (Dutch and German) Daddy

Poliklinik (German) Outpatient clinic

Polizeiliches Durchgangslager Westerbork (German) Police Transit Camp Westerbork

Putzkolonne (German) Cleaning crew (camp jargon)

'Raus (German) Out; get out (short for *heraus*)

Razzia (Dutch) A raid, roundup

Rivierenbuurt (Dutch) The River Area; an area of Amsterdam in which the streets are named after rivers.

Schleuse (German) Sluice; lock; process of registration, disinfection, etc., upon arrival in a concentration camp (camp jargon)

Schleusen (German) To sluice; theft that occurred during the registration process at a concentration camp (camp jargon)

Schnell (German) Quick; quickly

Seestrasse (German) Lake Street

Siechenheim (German) A hospital for incurables; in Theresienstadt, a "home" for the elderly and the sick

Sinterklaas or **Sint Nicolaas** (Dutch) Saint Nicholas, whose birthday festival is celebrated on December 5

Sponzendoos (Dutch) Sponge box, in which schoolchildren kept
the sponge and chamois to clean their slates

Strafbaracke (German), **Strafbarak** (Dutch) Punishment barracks

Tafelberg (Dutch) Table Mountain, the only "mountain" in Holland

Topfschlagen (German) To beat the pot; a children's game

Trakteren (Dutch) To treat; to stand treats

Traubenzucker (German) Grape sugar; glucose

Voor Joden verboden (Dutch) Forbidden to Jews

Wacht eventjes (Dutch) Wait a minute

Warenmagazin (German) *See* Magazin

**"Wer diese Quittung verfaelscht oder nachmacht oder
gefaelschte Quittungen in Verkehr bringt, wird strengstens
bestraft"** (German) "Whoever falsifies this note, alters it
fraudulently or imitates it, or whoever puts false notes into
circulation, will be severely punished" (text on banknotes used
in Theresienstadt)

Wim (Dutch) Masculine name

Zimmerdienst (German) Room duty, including cleaning of the
room

Zimmeraelteste (German) The elder of the room; person in a
concentration camp barracks who is in charge of a room

Zus (Dutch) Sis, short for *zuster*, sister

Zwarte (Dutch) Black; the Dutch police, who wore black uniforms

Zwarte Piet (Dutch) Black Peter, a Moor and helper to Sinterklaas

Notes

[1] Presser, J. *Ondergang—De Vervolging en Verdelging van het Nederlandse Jodendon.* 's Gravenhage: Staatsuitgeverij (1965), page 220 (English title: *Ashes in the Wind)*

[2] Boas, Jacob. *Boulevard des Misères.* Archon Books (1985), pages 4, 5

[3] Adler, H.G. *Theresienstadt 1941-1945—Das Antlitz einer Zwangsgemeinschaft.* Tuebingen: J.C.B. Mohr (Paul Siebeck) (1955), pages 29, 30, 31

[4] ibid, page 329

[5] Hofer, Hans "Der Film ueber Theresienstadt" in Hans Hofer, et al., *Theresienstadt.* Vienna: Europa-Verlag (1968), pages 194-199

[6] Adler, H.G. *Antlitz,* page 179

[7] —— *Die verheimlichte Wahrheit—Theresienstaedter Dokumente.* Tuebingen: J.C.B. Mohr (Paul Siebeck) (1958). Adler reprints several documents, used by Gerron, in this book.

[8] Hofer, Hans. "Der Film..." page 198

[10] Adler, H.G. *Antlitz,* page 179

[11] —— *Dokumente,* page 326

[12] —— *Antlitz,* page 180

[13] —— *Dokumente,* page 193

[14] ibid, page 209

[15] ibid, page 212

[16] ibid, page 213